INTERNATIONAL
HOTEL
REDESIGN

INTERNATIONAL
HOTEL
REDESIGN

Anne M. Schmid

Distributor to the book trade in the United States and Canada:
Rizzoli International Publications, Inc.
300 Park Avenue South
New York, NY 10010

Distributor to the art trade in the United States:

Letraset USA
40 Eisenhower Drive
Paramus, NJ 07652

Distributor to the art trade in Canada:

Letraset Canada Limited
555 Alden Road
Markham, Ontario L3R 3L5, Canada

Distributed throughout the rest of the world by:

Hearst Books International
105 Madison Avenue
New York, NY 10016

Library of Congress Cataloging-in-Publication Data

Schmid, Anne M.
    International Hotel Redesign / by Anne M. Schmid.
        p.   cm.
    Includes index.
    ISBN 0-86636-113-8
    1. Hotels, taverns, etc.—Conservation and restoration.
    2. Hotels, taverns, etc.—Remodeling   I. Title.
    NA7800.S36   1999
    728'.5'0286—dc20   89-9332
                                                    CIP

*CAVEAT—Information in this text is believed accurate, and will
pose no problem for the student or casual reader. However, the
authors were often constrained by information contained in
signed release forms, information that could have been in error or
not included at all. This refers specifically to the names of hotels,
designers, management companies, architects and
photographers. Any misinformation (or lack of information) in
these areas is the result of failure in these attestations. The
authors have done whatever is possible to insure accuracy.*

Color separation, printing and binding by
Toppan Printing Co. (H.K.) Ltd. Hong Kong
Typesetting by **Jeanne Weinberg Typography**

10 9 8 7 6 5 4 3 2 1

ACKNOWLEDGMENTS

*For their unyielding support, unselfish energy,
and unending loyalty, I am eternally grateful to
the following individuals in preparation of this
volume: my editors, Kevin Clark and Joseph Dionisio;
my art directors, Richard Liu and Daniel Kouw;
my friend and colleague, Steve Trombetti, Director of
Communications, American Hotel & Motel Association;
my consultant and patient husband,
Reinhold F. Schmid, president, Redesign, Inc.;
and most of all, the talented designers whose
outstanding work is presented on these pages.
To all of you—a heartfelt thanks!*

TABLE OF CONTENTS

FOREWORD

The rising popularity of hotel restoration, I believe, has several causes. Public consciousness and the search for our roots is part of a renewed pride in every major American city. This sense of history has given great old hotels, even the ones long neglected and derelict, a definite magic. Whether the National Trust realizes it, their focus on America's old structures has kindled appreciation across the land in our once great hotels in Richmond, Chicago, New York, Pittsburgh, Washington, San Francisco, St. Paul, Baltimore and Philadelphia. These scenes of local and national history commanded the best spot in town—usually the Center Square. Huge lobbies, "Peacock Alleys," great marble columns, grand stairways, Palm Courts and undeniable romantic presence dominated the environment.

Following World War II, the populace surged away from towns, while pushing shopping malls away from Main Street. Also, the decline of railroads—which brought business and travel to the heart of town, and thus to the big hotels—contributed to the neglect and fall of the central city. "Old-Fashioned" was as out-of-date as the "Student Prince" and the "Chocolate Soldier." But now the tide is rising and there is a move back to the center city, the rediscovery of the unequalled charm of historic buildings and especially grand old hotels.

Generous federal tax arrangements, of course, have for fifteen years encouraged builders to discern the buried gold in their historic structures. Even though, as usual, money is the lubricant. The most powerful force has been an American heart that longs for excellence and beauty in building palaces for people.

For a time the restoration was break-neck, pell-mell like the Gold Rush. Heedless enthusiasm tore into old buildings like Schliemann burrowing through precious archeological levels to find ancient Troy. Reckless decisions made way for air-conditioning ducts and "modern" plumbing. But with the rise to power of Landmark Associations, the white hats are on the scene to protect the treasure, and the engineers, architects and interior designers are now the heroes, sensitively rerouting pipes, conduits, flues, and electrical systems. Fine craftsmen—the plasterer, the gilt-leaf artist, the restorer of marble and stained glass, and the scagliola maker—are once again sought and rewarded. The remark that "There are no more skilled craftsmen" is simply not true. Restoration is now a major architectural discipline.

Consequently, research has become a consideration of time and budget. The interior designer begins his research not only with the study of the original floor plans and elevations (if the blueprints still exist), but also with the study of old photographs. This effort guides the way to carpet design, light fixtures, the history of the site, diaries, old clippings, historical societies and a reading of the community's attitude.

The challenge is to match the memories. Inevitably, there are torrents of mail: "My mother made her debut there... My wedding was in the Crystal Room... We danced on the roof... We met the President... Do you want the curved door to the old bar? I bought it at an auction but you can have it!... Please don't change anything."

Such fond memories of "the way it was" are the most difficult and sensitive aspects of restoration.

To reassure the memory while bringing the area into today's acceptable standards of lighting and palette is a designer's secret wizardry.

The designer literally lives with the part—like an actor learning his lines—then builds himself into the character. The public, in all cases, is waiting and grateful! The designer is charged with giving the public back its elegance, romance and history. The initial research, far from slowing down the design process, gives it a firm foundation and gives clues to the period, and even color.

All the symptoms of old age, however, are inherent in old buildings. These include weak structures, the hidden cancer of asbestos, dry rot, drafty windows that defy heating as well as air-conditioning, and tired, leaky plumbing. The encrustation of thoughtless additions must also be removed, likewise the devastating bad taste of other eras, grafted on the earlier structure.

Working on registered and/or certified buildings creates further design limitations. But, like having a demanding teacher or a strict disciplinarian, you often end up with a much better product for the rules. Other restrictions come from the owner's side, where creative design ideas face an ultimate test— those who are sometimes bent on preservation. When dealing with a bonafide treasure, there is no room for free-wheeling creative design. If they have an old wreck with no viable history, then indeed, it is time for imaginative design.

Existing casegoods have their own effect on a design. The search for old treasure is simply one of the most important and rewarding aspects of restoration. Many murals, discarded statues, beautifully framed paintings, early old couches, and massive lobby chairs are to be found in storerooms and basements. These, well restored, give flavor to the decor, if appropriate.

Important to the hotelier as well as the guests, the interior environment is the saleable, evident, unique factor for the hotel—the difference in this sometimes fierce competition. For the guest, it is simply The Experience.

Sarah Tomerlin Lee

INTRODUCTION

Grand hotels are back in style; in fact, they're setting the style.

Backed by the ample resources of international investors and monied moguls, hotels are again the places to see and be seen. Owners are more willing than ever to employ design minds and design materials that will make their properties stand out in an increasingly congested field. Whether in city centers or resort destinations, owners of major hotels want their properties to be showplaces, rather than cut-rate monuments to inhuman efficiency. Their desire to make their hotels "important" has led to a breathtaking game of creative one-upmanship, while propelling renovations (like the Biltmore's) onto the pages of slick magazines around the world. In essence, they have forged new visual standards for a highly visible industry.

It is precisely because the hotel industry is so visible that design is critical. By way of magazines, books, television and movies, the traveling public knows well what to expect from a great or even a good hotel. As city center hotels and fine resorts charge nightly rates skyrocketing past the U.S. $200 mark, guests are no longer overlooking tattered carpeting, faded linens and outmoded design. They know they can do better because they've read about the multi-million-dollar renovation of a nearby hotel. Failure to meet the guests' expectations opens the door for the competition. Simply put, hotels have no aesthetic margin for error.

Hoteliers are under almost unparalleled pressure to keep their properties looking perfect. More and more frequently, renovation is not a matter of "if" but of "when." Hotels that were renovated once every decade or two are now redesigned every five to seven years —not because modern design interiors are less lasting, but because every element of the design is closely monitored to insure it still "works."

As the range of projects in INTERNATIONAL HOTEL REDESIGN demonstrates, there is no single design solution to the challenge of redesign. Properties vary architecturally and geographically; they address different cultures and different markets. Art Deco works as well as Post-Modern when handled correctly. But, as all of these projects can attest, the trend is toward quality design and quality materials.

Another trend in renovation is the long-awaited move toward fully integrated design. Aesthetic makeovers for hotels are no longer designed piecemeal, with all of the money spent on the lobby. Equal attention is now being given to the guestrooms and other previously under-designed areas such as swimming pools, bars and banquet rooms. Since hotels must now turn a profit at every corner of available space, designers must create a look that invites guests to explore the entire property and make use of all its services. Renovation jobs offer designers and hoteliers the perfect opportunity to give an older hotel an integrated image. Bars and lounges can emerge from dark corners into the light of the lobby. These quiet retreats of the evening can be "lightened up" during the day, often as space to serve afternoon tea from gleaming silver trays. For early morning use, a flexible design can transform them into casual areas for a continental breakfast. Versatility is a key factor as hotel interiors are being rethought by today's designers.

Even lobbies are being redefined. Noisy, cold spaces are incongruous with the elegant yet quasi-residential formality of many of today's great hotels. Traditional check-in counters with multiple lines have been replaced by one-to-one check-in stations featuring curved wooden secretaries. Even in mega hotels, designers are renovating lobby space to provide individual, computerized check-in "pods" that allow for more personalized service.

As the projects in the following pages suggest, today's renovation and redesign doesn't always signal massive change. In many instances, they are actually closer to restoration. Is it difficult to return historic hotels to their original states because of modern safety requirements, but fortunately, there is a strong trend toward recapturing the property's original visual style, ambience and drama. This movement has helped forever erase the idea that renovation must mean aesthetic modernization. As designers now know, paneling over marble columns, or arranging vinyl butterfly chairs under a priceless Tiffany dome doesn't update a hotel's look; it only homogenizes it.

Designers involved in the renovation of classic hotels are finding ways to preserve the details that give a hotel its character. They invest large portions of their renovation budgets to save what is real—the chandeliers, architectural accents, wood panelings, etc. Then, with an eye to the bottom line, they may opt to reproduce seating that conveys the elegance of a bygone era—without paying the price for antiques. Here, too, design is integrated with the architectural shell to give guests a visually complete package.

Saving these great old hotels and giving them new life is as much a matter of pride as of necessity. This is especially true for established city centers, which have sites that are virtually priceless. Hotel companies appreciate their worth and, through renovation, are transforming these grand dames into flagship properties. The Chicago Hilton and Towers is a case-in-point. Originally, Hilton had plans to build a new hotel to replace the then 2,220-room Conrad Hilton. But, after talking with designers and estimating new construction costs, Hilton chose to undertake what was then the most expensive U.S. hotel renovation ever done (U.S. $185 million in 1985) and return the property to its showplace status. Now, with only 1,600 rooms and reformulated interiors, the Chicago Hilton and Towers competes successfully in a market in which six 5-star properties opened in two years, with several more under construction.

Renovation is more than simply rethinking existing hotel space. At times, it means rethinking the purpose of the space. Since prime sites are limited, post offices, hospitals, even factories may be the basis for a hotel. Such innovative, yet necessary views of redesign led to the conversion of a bullring in Zacatecas, Mexico; a highly successful hotel space comprised of four apartment buildings in Istanbul, Turkey; and the transformation of the Rambagh Palace from one of the world's largest residences to a palatial 5-star hotel.

Whether challenged by this kind of renovation or simply converting dull concrete-box construction into inviting, contemporary space, designers have used renovation as a springboard toward new design approaches.

Because they can see what doesn't work in a hotel, they have the opportunity to test new solutions. They can try a more residential look, strip away frills or add florals. From roadside motels being renovated to compete with new types of hotel products, to city center landmarks, renovated hotels look increasingly diverse, as the designs in this book make evident.

Although this is only a sampling of the thousands of hotel renovations undertaken each year, it reveals the industry's commitment to ongoing renovations and the new directions taken by interior designers who are making hotel interiors more dramatic and dynamic.

The designs within INTERNATIONAL HOTEL REDESIGN also underscore the importance of ingenuity and talent. Working within the constraints of existing spaces, and often mandated to utilize existing fixtures, these designers must use their skills to either enhance or remove elements. Their work will be measured directly against what was, and must measure up in the minds of guests. New construction offers designers an empty canvas; conversely, renovation invites comparison.

When that comparison is favorable, as it is for the projects within, the result is even more dramatic than a new opening. This aesthetic makeover generates

excitement—in the press, among previous guests and among those who may have only seen the outside of the hotel. A successful renovation literally creates a "new" hotel that can easily be positioned against new construction and marketed as a hotel to rediscover.

The quality of the ongoing renovation work in the hotel industry reflects a willingness to change, while improving the industry's health and prospects for the future. It insures that hotels will continue to be visual trendsetters that reflect the needs of their guests and the tastes of the era.

JAMES ALI

Mary Scoviak-Lerner

Arrowwood—A Radisson Resort

Alexandria, Minnesota, USA

Project location
Alexandria, Minnesota USA

Hotel company
Arrowwood—A Radisson Resort

Interior design
CSA (Contract Service Associates)—Peter Donahue/*Senior Designer*

Architecture
BWBR Architects

Lighting
Hallmark Lighting (*guestroom*)

Furniture
Trouvailles (*lobby*); **I.C.F.** (*lobby*); **Shelby Williams** (*Lake Cafe, meeting rooms*); **Wellesley Guild** (*Lake Cafe*); **Jeffco** (*Lake Cafe*); **Dereka** (*Lake Cafe*); **Charlotte Chair** (*Lake Cafe*); **Lowenstein** (*Lake Cafe*)

Wall covering
J. Josephson (*guestroom*)

Floor covering
Philadelphia (*guestroom, meeting room*)

Photography
Robert Knight

Minnesota, known as the land of 10,000 lakes, abounds with numerous resorts and get-away spots. Among its finest is the Arrowwood—A Radisson resort situated on 450 acres of the state's lush north woods.

Built in 1946 as a "Dude Ranch" on the scenic shores of Lake Darling, it was converted into a state-of-the-art recreational facility by private investors who added a 170-room hotel.

Purchased by Carlton Companies in 1976, the management at Radisson decided to change the feel of the property by making it more contemporary, open and sophisticated, while depicting its surroundings.

Not being an historic landmark yet worthy of preservation, the designers at CSA, Inc. were allowed the freedom to update and renovate the hotel without restrictions. A Scandinavian theme was chosen to reflect both the northern climate and predominant heritage of the region. Local history notes that Alexandria was visited by Viking explorers in days of yore.

Nancy Cowette of CSA, Inc., the Minneappolis-based design firm explains, "The interior design was tied into the existing architecture. The high, open-beam ceilings were preserved so as not to impede the view of the lake. A centrally located fireplace, which serves as a divider between the dining room and the lobby, was also retained to add coziness and privacy to both areas." The $3.5 million renovation included the upgrading of all 170 guestrooms and suites, meeting facilities, restaurants and lounges.

Light-colored tones of blue and rose were introduced in the upholstery, floor covering and accessories to compliment the Nordic decor. Wood carvings by local Scandinavian artisans were added to enhance the ethnic theme. The existing indoor pool area was refurbished. A new outdoor pool and a sundeck facility were added. The entire renovation was completed in two years.

Lobby (before).

Lake Cafe (before).

Light blue and rose tones in carpeting and walls add brightness to contemporary Scandinavian decor of lobby (after).

Wooden ceiling adds warmth and coziness to the seating area overlooking the lake in the Lake Cafe (after).

Ceramic Buffet in the Lake Cafe (after).

Floral pattern of carpeting in the meeting room reflects a Scandinavian design (after).

Meeting room (before).

Two views of the newly renovated indoor pool with adjacent seating area (after).

Indoor pool (before).

Aspen Country Inn

Aspen, Colorado USA

Project location
Aspen, Colorado USA

Hotel company
Village Resorts, Inc.

Interior design
Aiello Associates, Inc.—Louis P. Aiello/ASID; Julia L. Johnson/ASID
Allied Member

Photography
Robert Springgate

It isn't often that an interior designer has the opportunity to stamp his identity on a property more than once. Louis Aiello of Aiello Associates, Inc. did just that.

Built in 1965, the Aspen Country Inn became one of the most popular eating establishments in Aspen, Colorado. Its "old inn" atmosphere made it a popular place to stay for skiers and non-skiers alike. Suffering from deterioration and neglect, the inn was acquired by its current owners, Village Resorts, who wanted it restored to its former prominence by combining old world elegance with a comfortable, residential feeling.

Twenty-three years later, the Aiello design team was faced with several obstacles. According to the firm's president, Penny Aiello, "Time and budget constraints and keeping the hotel in operation while working on the restoration presented a problem." In addition, the designers were requested to use as many of the old furnishings as possible. These would eventually be replaced over a three-year period.

Original antique pieces, millwork and stained glass windows helped retain the atmosphere and ambiance of the old inn. A staircase and additional millwork were purchased from a Kansas City mansion.

One of the most popular areas, the den/library room, was converted from a former cocktail area. By retaining the fireplace and adding bookcases, comfortable seating and good lighting, the room attracts early morning newspaper readers as well as evening cocktail drinkers.

An "al fresco" atmosphere characterizes the Greenhouse dining room. Colorful floral wallpaper, a multi-colored slate floor and traditional wicker furniture create the "patio" effect.

Guestrooms were given a warm, homey feeling with the introduction of lace and patterned draperies and bedspread material. Armoires conceal the TV when not in use and house the electric coffee-maker and refrigerator.

Outdated bathroom vanities were updated with imported marble and brass hardware. Spaciousness was created with large mirrors framed by traditional maple moulding. Drapery skirts, placed below the vanity, offer additional storage area.

Greenhouse Dining Room (before).

Lace shirred tie-back curtains soften the windows overlooking the pool deck and mountain view (after).

Fireplace was retained to enhance coziness (after).

Den/library (before).

Entrances to the den/
library are accented by tie-
back drapes which are
drawn for private
functions (after).

Comfortable seating draws
guests from morning 'til
night (after).

Lace and patterned
draperies add homey
feeling to the guestroom **(after)**.

Typical guestroom (before).

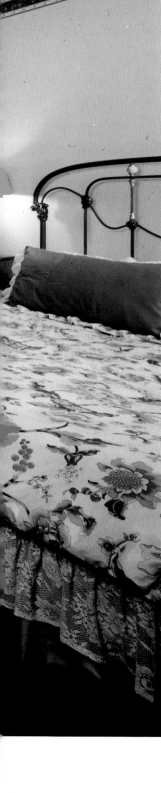

Bathroom vanity (before).

Wallpaper and border design were coordinated with the marble to create intimacy (after)·

Hotel Atop The Bellevue

Philadelphia, Pennsylvania USA

Project location
Philadelphia, Pennsylvania USA

Hotel company
Richard I. Rubin & Co.

Interior Design
Tom Lee Limited—Sarah Tomerlin Lee/*Conceptual Designer*;
Roger Danford/*Project Director*; **Alex Markowica**/*Architectural Designer*

Architecture
R.J.K.L. Associates, Inc.

Lighting
Louis Baldinger & Sons ; Albert Jaspers

Furniture: **Bibi Continental; Trouvailles; Wycombe-Meyer Co., Inc.; Tropi-Cal**

Floor covering
Avalon Commercial Corp. (*Conservatory floor tile*); **Elena Gordon/David Gordon Associates** (*carpet design*); **Edward Molina Designs** (*carpet manufacturer*); **BMK Carpets Limited** (*Ballroom carpet*); **Wilton Royal** (*guestroom carpets*)

Photography
Nathaniel Lieberman Studio Ltd.

The grand old Bellevue, which for nearly a century had been the center of entertaining, civic celebrations, and the pride of Philadelphia, was dealt a near fatal blow fifteen years ago with the tragedy of Legionnaires Disease. Scores of visiting guests were stricken, some fatally, ultimately forcing its closure.

The hotel was, in fact, two hotels originally. The Stratford Hotel and Hotel Bellevue were located across the street from one another in downtown Philadelphia. Upon purchasing them both in 1902, George C. Boldt decided to combine them into one. After a two-year U.S. $8 million construction program, the hotel opened its doors as the Bellevue Stratford on September 20, 1904.

The building was designed in the French Renaissance style and boasted "the most magnificent ballroom in the United States." Among the amenities and services offered were electric curling irons and coal-burning fireplaces in the guestrooms. Typists and stenographers were made available to the business clientele. Even a pet hotel was built on the roof to house the domesticated companions of hotel guests. Anyone who was anyone stayed at the Bellevue Stratford.

As years went by and numerous renovations dulled the glamour of the hotel's rich and decorative architectural style, its appeal began to wane. In 1976, the final curtain was drawn on the Bellevue in the aftermath of the epidemic disease.

The hotel had been closed for two years when developer Richard I. Rubin saw the potential in revitalizing the property. Upon acquiring the building, he negotiated a restoration with a California-based hotel chain, but with no results. Another international chain agreed to reopen the Bellevue after an extensive restoration—but again without success. Rather than give up, the Rubin company tried once more, this time converting the historic property into a mixed-use facility of shops and offices, capped off by a 173-room hotel on the top seven floors.

Sarah Tomerlin Lee, president of Tom Lee Ltd., the New York-based interior design firm, was approached to restore the "old Grande Dame of Broad Street." It took an inordinate amount of historical research and personal interviews, with individuals who remembered the Bellevue's days of glory, to form the design concept which would lead to her resurrection.

Because the hotel's credibility had been damaged, according to Ms. Lee, "Our chief objective was to win back the love and loyalty of the Philadelphians."

The Lee organization succeeded in restoring some of the most magical spaces in the hotel industry. The sixteen-foot arched windows of the circular Barrymore Room and Founders Club, which had been boarded up during previous renovations, again offer guests a dynamic view of the city. Exquisite murals, taken from a design developed for Napoleon III, grace the walls of the Rose Garden, a lovely small ballroom. But for Sarah Lee "the most thrilling space of all," she says, "is a sun-filled breakfast, lunch and cocktail terrace, located on the twelfth floor, which we discovered by eliminating eleven floors of dark guestroom space and opening the great area to skylights and a sky mural."

Ms. Lee notes, "Philadelphia has already taken the newest Bellevue to its heart." Well said by a true expert!

Ethel Barrymore would be pleased with the view of Philadelphia from the massive arched windows of the Barrymore Room, named after her theatrical family (after).

(before)

Ceiling detail of the Barrymore Room (after).

Murals, taken from a design created for Napoleon III, grace the walls of the Rose Garden Ballroom (after).

One of the most popular restaurants, the Conservatory, is enlivened with skylights and a domed sky mural (after).

Rose Garden
Ballroom (after).

Dark wood paneling adds
a club-like atmosphere to
the Philadelphia Library
Lounge (after).

Philadelphia Library
Lounge (before).

The Biltmore Hotel

Coral Gables, Florida USA

Project location
Coral Gables, Florida USA

Hotel company
The Sovereign Group

Interior design
Lynn Wilson Associates, Inc.—Lynn Wilson/*Principal;* **Gloria Calhoun, Jerry Szwed, Frank Cervoni; Joseph Herndon**/
Preservation Architect

Lighting
Hart Country Shop (*Biltmore Grill, Cafe, 7th Floor dining room*); **Carl Meyerson** (*guestrooms*); **Hart Associates** (*guestrooms*); **Chapman** (*7th Floor dining room*)

Furniture
J.J. World Trading Co. of Guatemala (*lobby, 7th Floor dining room*); **Antique Imports Warehouse** (*lobby*); **Rod Tuisan Antiques** (*lobby*); **Hammer of California** (*Biltmore Grill, 7th Floor dining room*); **Super Tak** (*Cafe*); **Martex** (*Cafe*); **Drexel Heritage** (*guestrooms*); **Georgian Reproduction** (*7th Floor dining room*); **IPF** (*7th Floor dining room*)

Wall covering
Blau Textiles (*7th Floor dining room*)

Floor covering
Regency (*Biltmore Grill, 7th Floor dining room*); **Forms and Surfaces** (*Cafe*); **Durkan** (*guestrooms*)

Photography
Karl Francetic Photography

Few of the hotels built in the United States during the first quarter of the 20th century can lay claim to the word "grand." This classification stemmed from European institutions such as The Ritz in Paris, the Conaught in London and the Sacher in Vienna.

Completed in 1926 as a tribute to eclectic Moorish, Spanish and Beaux Arts influences, the Biltmore in Coral Gables, Florida grew in just such a tradition. During her first 20 years she bathed her guests in comfort and grandeur. However, after being purchased by the federal government in 1947, the Biltmore became a part of the American war effort and was transformed into a hospital —offering comfort of a different sort.

Government standards had no need for elaborately painted ceilings, chandeliers, marble floors or other refinements. Roaches, rodents and homing pigeons contributed to the ignominious condition..

According to Lynn Wilson, president of Lynn Wilson Associates, Inc., "To comply with established government regulations, the polychromed lobby ceiling was transformed to a painted white plane; floors were covered with black linoleum; windows were reconfigured with aluminum framing; rooms were partitioned and given fluorescent fixtures."

The challenge was mammoth and problems unending. Faced with both time and budget constraints, and preservation requirements, the designers were asked to restore the Biltmore to its original elegance and grandeur.

Architects Leona d Schultze and Fullerton Weaver originally designed the hotel around a central 315 ft.-high tower replicating the Giralda tower in Seville, Spain. This area was bordered by two seven-story guestroom wings and function rooms surrounding the courtyard.

One of the obstacles encountered by the design team was to maintain the historical integrity of the building. New dining and ballroom facilities had to be created in areas which could not be spatially altered. The floors in each of the guestroom wings were gutted and the number of rooms reduced to 285 from the previous 350 in the east wing. A private dining club replaced the seventh floor guestroom wing. New windows and French doors were added throughout at the cost of U.S. $1 million.

Due to the lack of documentation and skilled craftsmen, the interior decoration offered the biggest challenge. The lobby ceiling, for example, had been altered by the addition of a sprinkler system. Ms Wilson notes, "Fortunately, vestiges of paint remained in the corners to provide the necessary color clues using microscopic analysis. Existing sepia-toned photographs of the original ceiling indicated its patterning." It required thirty-five Mexican ecclesiastical restorers to recreate the lobby's wall and ceiling.

In addition, the travertine floor had to be cleaned and the termite-infested oak veneer trim replaced with mahogany carved in Guatemala. Some furnishings and lighting fixtures were reproduced and custom-made. Materials were provided from 12 foreign countries.

Even with the original budget of U.S. $7.5 million cut in half midway through the project, the design team was able to return The Biltmore to its "grande dame" status after eight months of intensive labor.

Lobby (after).

Lobby (before).

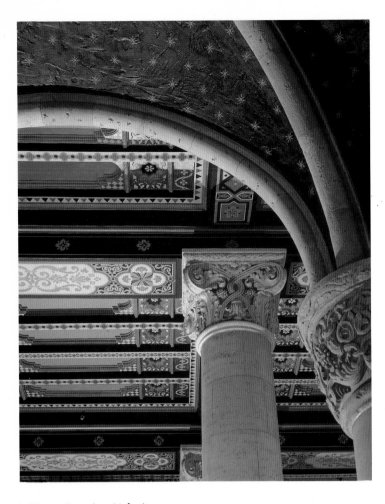

*Lobby ceiling detail (**after**).*

*What was once a laundry room is now the country style Cafe (**after**).*

Beaux-art eclecticism is evident in the furnishings of the "Biltmore Grill" (after).

A Spanish influence characterizes this typical bedroom. The Biltmore crest adorns the headboard (after).

Hues of coral and green complement the dark-stained mahogany millwork in the private dining room (after).

Marble floors were resurrected to enhance the beauty of the period furniture in the "Biltmore Grill" (after).

The Biltmore

Los Angeles, California USA

Project location
Los Angeles, California USA

Hotel company
Biltmore Partners

Interior decorator
Marcia Johnson

Architecture
Barnett Schorr Architects

Photography
No credit given

In 1922, ground was broken for what was to become the largest and most elaborate hotel west of Chicago. Upon opening, it was dubbed "the host of the coast." Conceived in Spanish-Italian Renaissance design by architects Schultze & Weaver (designers of The Biltmore in Coral Gables, Florida), it reflected the grand style of the 1920s. A lavish interior ceiling and wall paintings by famed Italian artist Giovanni Smeraldi added to the grand style of the 1,000-room property. In 1928, the hotel underwent a U.S. $4 million expansion, adding 500 guestrooms and a ballroom.

The Biltmore was updated in 1976 by owners/architects Phyllis Lambert and Gene Summers, who introduced contemporary furnishings, colors and art.

Purchased by Biltmore Partners in 1984, the hotel underwent a U.S. $40 million restoration to preserve its aesthetic and architectural beauty.

The original Music Room was converted into the new lobby which now features a marble fountain, overstuffed furniture and antique tables. An inlaid carpet lends accent to the marble-bordered wood floor. The focal point of the lobby is a 14-by-24 foot trompe l'oeil mural which depicts a 19th century garden court and park, beyond which is a view of the Los Angeles skyline.

In the Main Galeria, custom-designed rugs in floral patterns add emphasis to the 350-foot long marble walkway. Recessed lighting illuminates the vaulted ceiling and friezes, designed by Giovanni Smeraldi in the 1920s. These were carefully cleaned and treated with fresh colors and gold leaf. The original gold and green chandeliers were also restored.

Guestrooms have been refurbished in three major color schemes: pale yellow and gray lilac; rose; and light green. Furnishings include a mixture of traditional and French pieces.

In the Crystal Ballroom, which takes its name from two 12-foot wide crystal-lace chandeliers, the domed ceiling had to be washed with a special formula to remove nicotine and smog. A coat of buttermilk was applied to give the ceiling a uniform sheen and protect it from further damage.

In the Emerald Room, once the main dining room of the hotel, the hand painted ceiling of case plaster - decorated with dogs, rabbits, and roosters; was cleansed to freshen and highlight its vivid artwork.

In addition, a 24-story office tower was added to the existing building, as well as a new port cochere which services both the hotel and office tower.

The award-winning Biltmore has been named an "Historical Cultural Monument" by the Los Angeles Cultural Heritage Board.

Former Lobby (c. 1923) (before).

*The Rendezvous Court,
once the lobby of The
Biltmore, has been
converted to a lounge (after).*

The marble walkway of the Main Galeria is accented by custom designed multi-colored rugs in floral patterns (after).

The Main Galeria (c. 1923) (before).

The Olive Street entrance opens onto the Rendezvous Court (after).

The new lobby features a tromp l'oeil located behind the reception desk (after).

The Music Room (c. 1923) has been renovated into the hotel's lobby (before).

Boca Raton Hotel and Club

Boca Raton, Florida USA

Project location
Boca Raton, Florida USA

Hotel company
Arvida Corporation

Interior design
Lynn Wilson Associates, Inc.—Lynn Wilson/*Principal*; **Jerry Szwed**/
Project Architect; **Bruce Brockhouse**/*Project Architect*; **Terry Ruiz de
Castilla**/*Project Designer*

Lighting
Richard Ray Custom Design (*lobby*); **Frederick Cooper** (*Concierge
Lounge*); **Benson Lighting** (*Concierge Lounge*); **Trouvailles, Inc.** (*Court
of Four Lions*); **Remington** (*suite*); **Hart Associates** (*Court of
Four Lions*)

Furniture
Shelby Williams (*lobby, Court of Four Lions*); **Imports for the Trade**
(*lobby*); **Bernhardt Industries**(*Concierge Lounge*); **Georgian
Reproductions** (*Concierge Lounge*); **Drexel Heritage** (*Concierge
Lounge, Cloister Suite*); **Baker, Knapp & Tubbs** (*Concierge Lounge*);
Woodsmiths (*Court of Four Lions*); **Thomasville Furniture, Inc.**
(*Cloister Suite*)

Wall Covering
Wallco (*Cloister Suite*)

Floor Covering
Princeton (*Court of Four Lions*); **Duffy & Lee** (*Cloister Suite*); **Gilbralter**
(*Cloister Suite*)

Photography
Karl Francetic

Founded in 1897, the town of Boca Raton was a small
farming community whose original claim to fame was its
pineapples. Thirty years later it would become renowned
as a tribute to one man's vision. The man, Addison
Mizner—an architect and real-estate developer—dreamed
of building a community which would draw the well-
known and wealthy to its shores.

It was not enough to own an entire town. Mizner's
vision also included a hotel at its epicenter—a palace of
his own. The Cloister Inn, as it was then known, opened
its doors in February 1926. The property immediately
gained a reputation as being the most expensive
100-room hotel ever built—U.S. $1.25 million.

Spanish treasures and artifacts filled its rooms and
covered its walls—all selected by Mizner himself. A
20-lane highway, El Camino Real, was built to connect
the Cloister Inn with the city center. Unfortunately, it was
only a half-mile long at which point it funneled into a
two-lane dirt road. So much for grandeur!

No sooner had the hotel opened when the Great
Depression set in and Mizner, his wealth and health
depleted, was forced to abandon his dream community.

In 1928, Clarence H. Geist acquired the Cloister Inn
and renamed it The Boca Raton Hotel and Club.
Known for his eccentricity and ironclad rule, the property
was expanded to four times its size under his "reign."

Like several large hotels of the World War II era, the
Boca Raton was converted into an army barracks, albeit
the swankiest of its day. At war's end, noted hotelier J.

Myer Schine bought the hotel and had it completely
rehabilitated. Succeeding him in ownership was 88-year-
old Arthur Vining Davis, chairman of the board of Arvida
Corporation.

During the following years, a 25-story, 235-room tower
was completed and the 212-room Boca Beach Club
added. The total room count stood at 880.

Then in 1982 a tragic event occurred—the fabled Boca
Raton lost its 5-star rating. All stops were pulled to set the
queen back up on her pedestal. An intensive renovation
and restoration process was begun.

The 1920's Mizner-influenced design was brought back
to life by Lynn Wilson Associates. The firm's assignment
was to unify the traditional theme of the hotel and bring
order to disjointed interiors.

Upon entering the hotel, the mood for a traditional
environment is set by the magnificent arched ceilings in
the lobby and off the veranda. The Mizner-style castings
of Corinthian columns cap off the graceful arches. Such
1920's architecture dominates the total design of the
Boca Raton and most of its traditional pink facade.

Keeping with tradition and historic flavor, lighter colors
played a significant role. English chintz of floral paisley
complements lighter colors of peach, plum, mauve and
avocado accents. Guestrooms, suites, restaurants and
corridors were designed to retain architectural elements
as the focal point. Handcarved tables and delicate
antique vases were used throughout the public spaces.

The Boca Raton Hotel and Club can again boast a
5-star rating. Addison Mizner would be proud!

*Water fountain adds a
soothing elegance to
exterior of the Boca Raton
Hotel and Club (after).*

Exterior of The Cloister (before).

Interior veranda (before).

*Architectural details remain
the focal point in this
peach-toned dining area (after).*

A decidedly Spanish influence is noted in all facets of the lobby (after).

Lobby (before).

The beauty and elegance of the medieval-like Cathedral Dining Room are enhanced by the striking architectural detailing (after).

Floral window treatment contrasts well with green carpeting and upholstery, adding a regal touch to the Cloister Suite's parlor and bedroom (after).

Cloister Suite's parlor (after).

French doors allow natural light to filter into the Concierge Lounge (after).

The Broadmoor

Colorado Springs, Colorado USA

Project location
Colorado Springs, Colorado USA

Hotel company
El Pomar Foundation

Interior design
Wilson & Associates

Lighting
Craig Roberts Associates (consultant)

Floor covering
Larry Hokanson

Photography
Robert Miller

Recognized as one of the top resorts in the world, the 70-year-old Broadmoor lies at the foot of Cheyenne Mountain in southwest Colorado Springs.

The landmark complex, which covers an area of 2,000 acres, includes a convention center, eight restaurants, three golf courses, an ice rink, florist shop, greenhouse, service station and 550-room hotel.

The Broadmoor Hotel opened on January 29, 1918, immediately becoming the premier resort of the Rocky Mountains. It was owned for decades by the El Pomar Foundation, a charitable organization started by Spencer Penrose, founder of The Broadmoor.

Having fallen into disrepair over the past 70 years, the property was in dire need of renovation and upgrading. Wilson & Associates was commissioned to rejuvenate a number of suites and guestroom blocks as well as the lobby/reception area.

The "Penrose Suite" is one of the best examples of this magnificent facelift. According to Trisha Wilson, president of the Dallas-based design firm, "The challenge presented to us by the owner was to renovate the area while maintaining the integrity of its original timeless French design."

The suite itself incorporates several rooms: sitting room, living room, sun porch, kitchen, dining room, bathroom and three guestrooms. Access to the Penrose is achieved through a distinctive entry framed by two marble columns rising from a Versailles parquet floor.

A magnificent antique rock crystal and iron chandelier, serves as the focal point of the dining area.

Tones of soft salmon and moss green promote a warm relaxing atmosphere in the sitting and living rooms. An old world tapestry pattern was chosen for the armchairs in the sitting room while a custom-tufted rug adds interest to the original walnut hardwood floor in the living room.

Ms. Wilson notes, "We were careful in our selection of furniture to maintain the sophistication and elegance guests were accustomed to while introducing bright and lively color schemes." Consequently, both antique and reproduction furniture from the Louis XV and XVI eras are found throughout the luxury suite.

In the "Sun Lounge," the badly worn floor was replaced with tile and marble insets. The furniture chosen for this room includes a blend of rattan, twist chairs and upholstered sofas. Custom-made lamps, imported from France, enhance the ambience. An old fountain, which once graced the middle of the room, was removed to allow patrons an unobstructed view of the lake and adjacent mountains.

The award-winning redesign of the Broadmoor has re-established the resort's former reputation as the "Riviera of the Rockies."

Marble columns frame the entry to the Penrose Suite (after).

Entry to Penrose Suite (before).

The original walnut
hardwood floor showcases
a custom-tufted rug in the
Living Room (after).

Living Room (before).

The parquet top dining table is French walnut with dining chairs and console finished in desert crackle (after).

Dining Room (before).

The Sun Lounge (before).

The Sun Lounge is set off by its dramatic iron chandelier (after).

Carlton Suite Sitting Room (before).

Lounge chairs and throw pillows are covered in a rose-cream-and-green ribbon stripe in the Sitting Room (after)

Cairo Marriott Hotel

Cairo, Egypt

Project location
El Gezira Island, Cairo, Egypt

Hotel company
Marriott Corporation

Interior design
Edward Dann Design International—Edward C. Dann

Architecture
Frizzell Hill Moorhouse Architects—Ken Frizzell, Debra Lynn

Lighting
Craig Roberts Associates (consultant)

Photography
Wm. Kenneth Frizzell; Edward C. Dann; Charles Allison

What do you do when you have the Emperor and Empress of France coming over for dinner and no place to seat them? You build a palace! As Wm. Kenneth Frizzell of Frizzell Hill Moorehouse Architects puts it, "The history of the Palace is like a story from 'The Arabian Nights'."

Khedive Ismail had the Palace built in 1869 on Gezira Island, in the middle of the Nile, to entertain Napolean III and Empress Eugenie during the opening of the Suez Canal. According to Frizzell, "It contained three Palaces in separate wings—each in a different style. The wing housing the Imperial couple was a second Empire extravaganza. It contained a throne room reached by a fabulous staircase. The Khedive had the garden wing which was decorated in a garish Parisian-Islamic style. The third wing was a sedate Louis XV."

Commissioned by Marriott Corporation and the Egyptian government to restore the Palace, Frizzell was overwhelmed by the amount of deterioration and decay he found. He continues, "When I first saw it in 1974, it had deteriorated to near collapse. The ceiling of the throne room was about to cave in due to water leakage. Several remodelings had ruined the Nile Entrance and turned it into a truck dock and garbage dump. Huge rats were running around the parquet and marble floors."

Needless to say, much historical research had to be done to envision the grandeur which once existed. Edward Dann of Edward Dann International, the interior designer, states, "I learned that the Palace was designed by two Italian architects who, with the help of French and German designers and fabricators, developed the majority of the components used in the erection and furnishing of the building, in Europe. Remaining to this day are fine examples of Baccarat crystal chandeliers, European porcelains, hand-carved furniture, marble sculptures and mosaics."

It took eight years to restore the once grand structure. The core of the Palace, originally servants' quarters, was unsalvageable due to rot and had to be demolished. Because the floor to floor height was approximately 30 feet, a new four-story building was built within and topped off with a roof garden restaurant/nightclub. The "Golden Porch" entrance was built from bits of ornamental iron porches found scattered in other areas and reassembled. Furniture and pieces of sculpture were catalogued, repaired, restored and repositioned.

Even though the architectural and interior design team was able to resurrect much of the structure and artifacts, some were beyond rescue. Frizzell says, "A great marble staircase was lost in the rotted core and a mysterious grotto in the garden could not be saved."

Viewing the imperial splendor of the Cairo Marriott now, even Napolean would raise a toast to the two men responsible for its rebirth!

"Golden Porch" Nile entrance after construction.

Lobby and Staircase (before).

A mix of Islamic and French decor defines the Lobby and Staircase (after).

Interior Corridor (before).

Restored furnishings add
royal touch to Interior
Corridor (after).

Original museum quality paintings can be found in the Lounge and many other areas of the Palace (after).

Green upholstered chairs accent the green-and-white checkered marble tiles of the Ballroom (after).

Caledonian Hotel

Edinburgh, Scotland

Project location
Edinburgh, Scotland

Hotel company
Norfolk Capital Group PLC

Interior design
MIA Design—Elise Ide/*Interior Designer*; **Bob Mousley**/*Architect*;
Willie Atkins/*Architect*; **Philip McLean**/*Architect*

Architecture
MIA Design

Lighting
R & S Robertson (*fittings*)

Furniture
Figli di Adamo Busnelli

Floor covering
Mercia Weavers; Gavin Hamilton

Photography
Art Contact

In the land of kilts, bagpipes, the Loch Ness monster
and bonnie lads and lassies, lies a city to which even the
British royals flock—Edinburgh, Scotland. And in the
shadow of its more renowned structure, Edinburgh
Castle, stands a treasure of a property—the Caledonian
Hotel.

Famous for its rose pink sandstone facade, the 5-star
hotel was originally owned and constructed by the
Caledonian Railway Company in 1903. It was built on
the site of the original railway station and to this day
retains many distinctive station features.

To maintain its prominent position in the
heart of the Scottish capital, it needed to be upgraded.
MIA Design was approached by the Norfolk Capital
Group, its current owner, to renovate the existing
guestrooms whose features had grown out of date. A
period style was selected as the theme for the project
while introducing bright colors for a contemporary look.
According to Elise Ide, the project designer, "With high
ceilings, original cornices and large windows, the
bedrooms needed the decorative grand style of a period
room."

Some of the more challenging spatial obstacles were
the existing small single rooms. Bathrooms were separate
and remote from guestrooms and plumbing stacks
exposed.

The England-based design team solved these problems
by combining two single rooms into one long, narrow
double room. The plumbing was re-arranged to
incorporate baths into the guestrooms and concealed the
unsightly pipework with decorative pilasters. The
problem of different floor levels was turned into an
advantage by creating split-level suites.

The entire renovation was completed in two phases over
the course of one year. Twenty-seven rooms were
refurbished during the first six months and thirty-one
during the last six.

Presidential Suite (before).

Presidential Suite prior to renovation (before).

Blue and salmon color scheme adds a contemporary look to the living room and bedroom areas of the Presidential Suite (after).

Salmon-colored molding lends character to updated bathroom (after).

Bathroom (before).

Two views of typical single room (before).

Two small rooms are combined, allowing enough room to accommodate a desk and sitting area in a double room (after).

Canterbury Hotel

Indianapolis, Indiana USA

Project location
Indianapolis, Indiana USA

Hotel company
C & I Associates

Interior design
Morris Nathanson Design, Inc.—Morris Nathanson/*President*; **Peter A. Niemitz**/*Vice President*; **Blase Gallo**/*Vice President-Director of Design*; **Neil Pereshula**/*Vice President Production*

Architecture
Browning Day Mullins Dierdort Inc.

Lighting
Chapman Mfg. Co.; Metropolitan Lighting; Frederick Cooper

Furniture
Wycombe-Meyer; Trouvailles, Inc.; Chairmasters Inc.

Wall covering
MDC Walls Wallcovering

Floor covering
Navan Carpets

Photography
Greg Murphy

Afternoon tea, long a British tradition, has become a staple of life at the Canterbury Hotel in Indianapolis. This wasn't always the case. Prior to its current ownership, the hotel had the misfortune of being passed around like the proverbial "hot potato." It had been built and rebuilt, sold and resold, named and renamed so often that it suffered an identity crisis.

The original building, the Oriental Hotel, had been designed and erected in 1858 by architect Francis Costigan. After changing hands, it was renamed Mason House and later Oxford Hotel. In 1928 it was torn down to make room for a new 12-story, 200-room hotel named Hotel Lockerbie—the last hotel built in Indianapolis before the Depression. Indeed, the location was ideal, allowing the hotel to draw clientele from the bustling Union Station nearby.

In the early 1930s, hotelier Glen Warren acquired the property and proceeded to name it after himself. The Warren Hotel was sold in 1959 to the Boss Hotel chain but the name remained the same. By 1973, the property, suffering from inferior management and neglect, was forced to close.

Next came developer George Ginger, who bought the Warren in 1980 fully intending to convert it into an apartment complex. However, difficulty in obtaining financing forced him to abandon the project.

Finally, in 1983, three investors, Fred Tucker, Gunnar Nilsson and Donald Fortunato purchased the orphaned building hoping to resurrect it as a world class business hotel.

Morris Nathanson Design, Inc., was approached to convert the historic landmark into a luxury property. A problem arose. Nathanson explains, "Strict guidelines had to be adhered to so the owners could apply for historic   tax credits. The biggest obstacle to overc[ome]   any diverse design styles and detail[s]   creating a traditional Englis[h]   every period was repre[sented]   had undergone many renovations over the years." The design team soon realized that there wasn't much left to preserve. For example, they discovered that the elaborate woodwork was actually plastercasting. The building had to be gutted almost entirely.

The brick and terra cotta facade was in the best shape of all requiring only a cleaning and installation of new windows.

He continues, "Planning a space took a great deal of consideration. The existing layout would not work for new uses." New plumbing, electrical and fire systems had to be installed and state-of-the-art elevators added. Rooms were combined to create doubles and bi-level penthouse suites. Flooring and architectural details were retained where possible. Many furniture pieces were customized to allow for greater unity in the overall design. Artwork and artifacts were carefully chosen to further unify the spirit of tradition and elegance.

A new, two-story atrium is now used for various social functions. In the Parlor guests can relax in an English sitting room complete with carved wooden fireplace and library.

The Canterbury now stands as a tribute to English tradition in the finest sense of the word.

Atrium Lobby (before).

The central court of the
Atrium Lobby serves as a
function room for various
events (after).

Typical guestroom (before).

Comfortable furniture in the guestroom parlor offers relaxation throughout the day (after).

Floral bed cover and drapes add an elegant coziness to the bedroom (after).

The wood paneling and fireplace of the Sitting Room are reminiscent of an old gentleman's club (after).

Hyatt Carlton Tower

London, England

Project location
London, England

Hotel company
Hyatt Corporation International

Interior design
Hirsch/Bedner & Associates—Howard Hirsch, Stephanie Hayes, Howard Pharr III

Architecture
DRS Associates

Floor covering
Wiltshier Interiors Limited; Tai Ping Carpets

Photography
Derry More (*phase 1*); **Jaime Ardilles-Arce** (*phase 2*)

By British standards, the hotel now referred to as the Hyatt Carlton Tower is a youngster among "grand" hotels. Built in the early '60s as a traditional luxury hotel, it had the misfortune of having several owners. The lack of continuity had a negative effect resulting in neglect and loss of stature.

Its location, in the heart of Belgravia, overlooking the gardens of Cadogan Place and Buckingham Palace, was ideal. But the competition was stiff with the likes of the Claridge, Savoy, Dorchester and the Ritz nearby.

Upon acquiring the management contract in the early 1980s, Hyatt International's intent was to convert the property into their flagship hotel for expansion into Europe, Africa, and the Middle East. However, the Carlton Tower was in desperate need of a facelift first.

Hirsch/Bedner & Associates of California was commissioned to upgrade and rehabilitate the hotel to regain its former elegance. Howard Hirsch's objective was to maintain the residential feel of the hotel, yet give the space a chic, contemporary look.

The first phase of the refurbishment program included the entry hall, Chinoiserie Tea Lounge, reception and concierge areas.

Working around the clock, the entire original entry hall was stripped in just five weeks. It was important to keep the hotel operational during the renovation process. The design team totally reconstructed the public areas, installing inward curving walls detailed in English sycamore paneling. Skilled craftsmen inlaid the custom-designed floor with Italian travertine marble. Traditional elegance was established through custom furnishings and authentic fine art and antiques collected from the Orient by Hirsch himself.

Three porticos, detailed with marble bases and wood cornice features, define the Chinoiserie Tea Lounge. Color tones of seafoam green, rose and jade add a subdued yet contemporary look. A gold silk fabric wall covering provides a warm background for Chippendale sofas, chairs and mahogany tea tables.

The second phase attended to the refurbishment of the Rib Room and the addition of a state-of-the-art health club. The restaurant was completely redesigned into three dining levels. On the lower one, for example, marble floors and banquettes accent imported Japanese tiles which create a pattern behind the cooking display area.

A new health club, The Peak, was added onto the roof of the east wing. Computerized exercise machines, saunas, and UVA sunbeds are among the many features offered at the premier facility.

Physical improvements and careful management have re-established the Hyatt Carlton Towers as a force among the premier hotels in London.

Detailed English sycamore paneling and travertine marble floor add traditional elegance to the Registration area of the lobby (after).

Lobby (before).

Amber lacquered
architectural elements
create a warm background
for the Chippendale
furnishings of the Chinoiserie
Tea Lounge (after).

Rib Room (before).

The cooking display area is highlighted by copper and rust colors on the lower level of the Rib Room (after).

Light colors and contemporary furnishings provide a refreshing, airy feeling in the Club Lounge of the new health club (after).

Casino de Deauville

Deauville, France

Project location
Deauville, France

Interior Design
Hirsch/Bedner International, Ltd.—Bob Bilkey; Oscar Llinas

Lighting
Lightsource; Bakalowitz; Legend Studios

Furniture
Marmi Formigari; Legend Studios; Metafer; Steve Gomley & Associates; Traditional Imports; Bibi Contract; Societe Coulombs; Wicker Works

Floor covering
Marmi Formigari; Bell Carpets; Kofra Ltd.

Photography
No credits given

The Duc de Mornay was not about to let his being the illegitimate half-brother of Louis Napoleon Bonaparte stand in the way of success. The resounding popularity of Deauville, the seaside resort he founded and developed in the 19th century, remains a testament to his foresight and creativity.

In the beginning, the sophisticates of Paris and London were drawn to the Hippodrome de la Touques, a race track built by de Mornay in 1862. After the turn of the century, a new attraction, the Casino de Deauville, was constructed by Eugene Cornuche for the well-heeled to enjoy.

Its popularity, however, eventually contributed to its decline. As the property became worn and outdated, the current owners, Les Hotels Lucien Barriere, soon realized that a facelift was needed to restore the casino to its original splendor.

Hirsch/Bedner & Associates, headquartered in Santa Monica, California, were given the assignment to return the Casino de Deauville to its former stateliness. The owner's chief concern was that an American design team would approach the design with Las Vegas "glitz." His fears were soon put to rest. After extensive research, the London-based members of the design company settled on the romantic charm of France's Belle Epoque era for inspiration.

It was important that the best elements of the past be retained while blending in a contemporary casino design. A slot-machine salon, the Salle de Machine a Sous, a first for the casinos of France, was gingerly incorporated into the interior yet made appealing with a variety of neon lights.

A palette of rose welcomes guests into the grand salon, where the entry is flanked by a dual staircase. A sparkling crystal chandelier adds a rich glow to the specially designed rose marble and hand-loomed custom carpets.

Smaller salons situated to the left and right of the entry lead to meeting areas and a variety of boutiques, restaurants and lounges. Handsome, handpainted murals and a stained glass ceiling highlight the intimate restaurant Les Cafe de la Boule. The focal point of the Salle de Jeux is a spectacular gazebo, "Temple d'Amour." Here one can either play at its European and American roulette tables, or enjoy a meal in Le Banco, a gourmet restaurant.

The sophisticates of Paris and London continue to flock to Deauville, as they did 100 years ago, but now they have to make room for the rest of the world.

Exterior of the Casino De Deauville (after).

*A wrought-iron and marble staircase flanks the new entry into the casino (**after**).*

*Hand-loomed custom carpets and crystal chandeliers add elegance to the Grand Salon (**after**).*

Le Cafe de la Boule is highlighted by handsome, handpainted murals and a stained glass ceiling (after).

A spectacular gazebo, "Temple d'Amour," serves as the focal point in the Salle de Jeux where roulette tables abound (after).

Etched glass partitions give diners a feeling of privacy in Le Banco, a gourmet restaurant (after).

Stunningly designed neon lights give an upbeat look to the Salle de Machine a Sous (after).

Chicago Hilton and Towers

Chicago, Illinois USA

Project location
Chicago, Illinois USA

Hotel company
Hilton Hotels Corporation

Interior design
Hirsch/Bedner & Associates

Architecture
Solomon, Cordwell, Buenz & Associates

Lighting
Wheel—Gersztoff

Furniture
Shelby Williams (chairs); **A. Rudin** (sofas)

Wall covering
Josephson, Inc.; Canovas, Manuel Canovas

Floor covering
Couristan (custom); **Tai Ping Custom Area Carpets**

Photography
Jaime Ardilles-Arce

Among the many things that Chicago prides itself on is its unique and varied architecture. So it was no surprise that James W. Stevens decided to build the 3,000-room Stevens, billed as the "greatest hotel" of its time, in this metropolis. The close proximity of Lake Michigan and its splendid lakefront parks, adjacent museums and surrounding nightlife, drew guests from around the country and the world.

Fifty years later, the Chicago Hilton and Towers (as it is now called) retains the same reputation. Having undergone a mammoth U.S. $185 million restoration/renovation in 1985, it now boasts one of the most expensive facelifts in hotel history.

Mr. Stevens envisioned the hotel as a city within a city. Upon completion in 1927, it offered convention facilities; a hospital; a laundry plant; a 1,200-seat theatre; a 27-chair barber shop; a five-lane bowling alley; a roof-top miniature golf course, a children's playroom, and on, and on, and on.... It was a fitting tribute to self-sufficiency and hyperbole.

The original design concept was considered one of the most ambitious construction undertakings of its time. The plans called for a Grand Ballroom completely free of visible structural supports. Four enormous steel trusses were constructed to compensate for the absence of 55 structural pillars. They also had to be of sufficient strength to support 22 stories of building above.

The interior design was decidedly French and luxurious, from the splendid bronze and crystal chandeliers to the stairs of imported Belgian marble.

During World War II, the hotel was requisitioned by the U.S. government and turned into a troop barracks and training facility. Its furnishings and equipment were auctioned off and the interior downscaled to meet with governmental standards.

After the war, the mega property was acquired by Conrad Hilton. Forty years later, Hilton executives decided to rebuild the outdated hotel and reclaim its position as one of the premier convention hotels of the world.

The rehabilitation included gutting the entire hotel, restoring its historic and irreplaceable design elements, and adding a seven-story building for parking, exhibit space and health club.

Hirsch/Bedner & Associates, the interior designers, were faced with returning an aura of grandeur to a mammoth structure while employing traditional architectural design. The lobby's ceiling mural and Italian marble columns were meticulously hand-restored by the Italian-born artisan Lido Lippi. Suspended on scaffolding, Michelangelo-style, 36 feet above the floor, it took him seven months to recreate the mural.

The guestroom total was reduced by almost half—to 1,620—as many of the original rooms were converted into multi-room suites. Others were combined to enlarge existing guestrooms. Solid cherry-wood and Hepplewhite furnishings add a residential feeling of comfort and relaxation. Bathrooms feature Italian marble floors and brass fixtures.

Among its imperial suites, the Conrad Hilton Suite is the most outstanding. Located on the 29th and 30th floors, it was converted from two smaller ballrooms. With three bedrooms, five bathrooms, a dining room which seats twelve, a library, fireplace, living salon and kitchen, it is literally a "home away from home."

Mr. Stevens would be proud to know that his dream is being kept alive at the Chicago Hilton & Towers.

Two stone sculptures,
which adorned the entry to
the old Stevens Hotel, now
add to the decor of the
dynamic Marble Hallway (after).

Marble Hallway (before).

Stone sculpture detail (after).

Lakeside Green (before).

The Lakeside Green atrium lounge offers a relaxing atmosphere to its patrons for Afternoon Tea or before-dinner cocktails (after).

A 17th century Flemish tapestry graces the wall above the dining area (after).

Marble-top bar and red upholstered stools complement the African wood paneling in Buckingham's (after).

Oak Room (currently Buckingham's Restaurant) (before).

Entry Foyer to Conrad Hilton Suite (after).

Fireplace adds coziness to the library/den of the Conrad Hilton Suite (after).

Two small ballrooms were combined into the Conrad Hilton Suite (before).

*French decor of the Grand
Ballroom Foyer is
reminiscent of the Palace
of Versaille (after).*

Twenty-two karat gold leaf was applied to the ornate walls and carvings of the Grand Ballroom (after).

A swimming pool is one of several features offered in the new health club facilities.

Equinox Hotel

Manchester Village, Vermont USA

Project location
Manchester Village, Vermont USA

Hotel company
Equinox Development Corporation/Galesi Group

Interior design
Dorothy Draper & Company—Carleton Varney/*Principal Designer*;
Charles R. Davis/*Project Designer*; **Dan Parker**/*Director of Design*

Architecture
Einhorn, Yaffee, Prescott, Krouner

Furniture
Romweber

Floor Covering
Dorothy Draper & Company

Photography
Billy Cunningham

To spend time at the Equinox Hotel is to step back in time. The historic inn once served as a summer retreat for the well-to-do Easterners of the Victorian era. Several U.S. presidents were known to have sought recreation and relaxation at this New England retreat, discreetly located at the foot of Mt. Equinox in Vermont. Abe Lincoln's family grew so fond of the surroundings and service that an entire suite was built especially for them.

When first constructed in 1769, the property was known as Marsh's Inn. After the American Revolution it came under new ownership and was rechristened Munson's Inn. Changing hands again, it was renamed Widow Black's Tavern.

It wasn't until 1853, when Franklin Orvis purchased the property, that the Equinox reached its "grand hotel" status. The privileged and their families could often be found fishing and bathing in the Battenkill River, strolling through the rich green forests or simply socializing on the veranda.

However, as many neglected old properties are wont to do, the landmark hotel started to deteriorate and was closed in 1974. Ten years and U.S. $20 million later, the Equinox was again reincarnated.

Carlton Varney, president of Dorothy Draper & Co., a New York-based interior design firm, was faced with reconstructing an era gone by. Through laborious research and the help of the Vermont Historic Preservation Office, he was able to recreate the Victorian and American Empire style which once graced the property.

Apart from the introduction of contemporary meeting facilities, a modern visual aid system and computer rooms, a characteristically Victorian aura was maintained. Red and green velvet and striped brocade upholstery add elegance to the early American Empire furnishings. Old turn-of-the-century bathroom sinks and porcelain faucets were reglazed. Pinewood furnishings enhance a charming country-look in the 144 renovated guestrooms.

Once used only as a summer and fall resort, the Equinox is now open all year. Ski enthusiasts converge to take advantage of the slopes in Vermont's Taconic mountain range and sleighs transport those less athletically inclined.

A two-story colonnade graces the entrance of the hotel (after).

Large windows add a residential charm in this typical guestroom (after).

A Victorian look is achieved with velvet and brocade upholstery, characteristic of that era(after).

Lobby (before).

An expansive bay window and white furnishings create a patio atmosphere in the 3,600 sq. ft. Dining Room (after).

Dining room (before).

Bar-Tavern (before).

Original pinewood plank flooring, accented by red and black checkered wallpaper and swag window treatment, reinforce an Early American look in the Bar-Tavern (after).

Hansa-Hotel

Kulmbach, West Germany

not just meet a hotel guest's basic needs but will insure them an experience not to be soon forgotten.

Project location
Kulmbach, West Germany

Interior design
Dirk Obliers Design GmbH

Carpentry
Friedhelm Hübner

Photography
Dirk Obliers

Nestled among the rolling hills and forests of northeastern Bavaria, lies the charming, historic city of Kulmbach. Surrounded by medieval castles and quaint little villages, it was the center of culture and commerce during the reign of its regional sovereign, the Prince of Kulmbach. Martin Luther, Richard Wagner and Goethe, three of Germany's elite, were also known to have had close ties to the area.

Currently renowned for brewing some of the best beer in the world, the city boasts another attraction—the Hansa-Hotel Kulmbach. Built in 1962 by Max Hoensch, the traditionally decorated interiors remained untouched for many years.

It became evident to the owners that a total renovation was required to continue its reputation as a hotel of choice for business travelers. Dirk Obliers Design was retained by Hoensch's daughter and grandson, Hannelore and Andreas Zollfrank, to give the property a contemporary look. According to Obliers, the most significant challenge he faced was "to combine the already existing name 'Hansa' with the interior design, thereby furnishing the hotel with a new corporate identity."

Between the 12th and 17th centuries, a string of independent cities formed a powerful economic community in northern Europe called "The Hanse." One of these cities, Breslau (currently Wroclaw, Poland) was the hometown of Mr. Hoensch, the hotel's founder, who adopted the name for his property. Taking the prevailing Gothic style of this period and abstracting the shape of the typical gabled roof, Obliers integrated the geometric pattern into the design theme.

The selected motif dominates all aspects of his design and is evident in two and three dimensional forms throughout. Obliers notes, "It is a shape that can easily be found framing the entry into the restaurant, repeated on the front of the registration desk or outlining the head of the bed in the guestrooms." A stylized version of the recurrent pattern also surrounds the multi-functional desks found in each room. These feature a pull-out corian desk top and built-in refrigerated minibar.

Obliers' wonderfully innovative and unique approach to design has insured the Hansa-Hotel's successful future. He prides himself on creating an environment which will

Old registration desk and foyer (before).

Restaurant (before).

*A view of the new bar
from the restaurant area (after).*

Interior view of the restaurant (after).

A typical single room (before).

Indirect lighting emphasizes the geometry of the unique design concept (after).

A typical double room (before).

The "Hansa" theme is repeated in the backboard of the double bed (after).

*Red accessories add spark
to the modern white-tiled
bathroom (after).*

Planters and room dividers
provide dining guests with
privacy from the activity in
the adjacent foyer (after).

Hyatt Regency Hong Kong

Kowloon, Hong Kong

Project location
Kowloon, Hong Kong

Interior design
Morford & Company Ltd.—John Morford/*Design and Detailing*;
Sam Lee/*Senior Project Assistant*

Lighting
ERCO; May Sun

Furniture
Cheng Meng; Hong Kong Teakwood; Shelby Williams (*lobby and cafe chairs*)

Wall covering
Pacific Decor; Source Interiors; T. Murakami

Floor covering
Tai Ping Carpets Ltd. (*guestroom and public area carpets*)

Photography
David Liu

Traveling up Nathan Road from the Hong Kong Space Museum towards Kowloon Park, the Hyatt Regency Hong Kong looms over Kowloon's colorful shopping, entertainment and business district.

Built twenty-five years ago, the 723-room hotel had already undergone a cosmetic rehabilitation process in the 1970s but lacked a cohesive design.

In 1984, John Morford of Morford & Co. Ltd., was approached to put together a design concept which would incorporate the entire property. Having been trained in the United States and already experienced in hotel design in the Far East, Morford brought with him the understanding of and appreciation for the melding of Western and Eastern cultural styles.

In preparing for the renovation, Morford's research unearthed a wealth of Chinese art which had been hidden away in closets and suites of the hotel. Rather than ignore the priceless collection, he decided to incorporate it into his design.

The design team soon discovered that restructuring an existing property can be more challenging at times than building a hotel from scratch. To keep guest discomfort at a minimum, three floors were worked on at a time. In addition, their attempt to raise ceilings in some of the public spaces, for a more elegant effect, was hampered by the city's height restrictions. As construction commenced, they luckily discovered circular sunken panels in the ceiling of the first floor which had been concealed during previous refurbishments. By uncovering the spherical coffer and applying a white plaster treatment, the ceiling was raised and converted into an architectural focal point.

Integration of Italian and Spanish marbles, natural teak wood paneling and halogen lighting established the lobby's status as the centerpiece of the hotel. Design elements such as black lacquer inlays, teak panels, brass, and beveled glass, complement the newly discovered Chinese artifacts which are found throughout the interiors.

The simple yet elegant design of The Chinese Restaurant won the "Best Restaurant" award from *Restaurants & Institutions* magazine and "Gold Key Award Grand Prize" from the American Hotel & Motel Association.

This balance of classical and modern styles, from the public areas to the guestrooms, has made the Hyatt Regency Hong Kong one of the choice hotels in Kowloon.

Lobby (before).

Three gold-leafed Taoist gods welcome arriving guests at the front desk in the lobby (after).

Theatrical lighting, teak wood paneling and exquisite antiques create an aura of understated elegance in the lobby lounge (after).

The Nine Dragons
Ballroom has been
replaced by The Chinese
Restaurant and Nathans (before).

The entrance to Nathans,
an enclosed streetside
dining area (after).

The Chinese Restaurant
balances classical and
modern styles while
creating a refined
atmosphere (after).

A private dining room in
The Chinese Restaurant (after).

Circular coffer ceiling adds drama to the Cafe Restaurant (after).

Teak wood and glass
partitions add privacy
to booths (after).

The Coffee Terrace (before)
has been replaced by the Cafe
Restaurant (after).

Hotel Inter-Continental New York

New York, New York USA

Project location
New York, New York USA

Interior design
Joseph Gruszak Associates—Joseph Grusczak; Inter-Continental Hotels Corporation Dept. of Interior and Graphic Design

Architecture
William B. Tabler

Lighting
Louis Baldinger & Sons (lobby chandeliers, surface light fixtures and sconces in guestrooms); **Norman Perry** (lamps); **Frederick Cooper** (guestroom lamps)

Wall covering
Hines/Charterhouse Designs, Ltd.; Maharam Fabrics; Design Tex

Floor covering
BMK Carpets; Navan Carpets, IDCNT-Center One; Carpets of Worth

Photography
Norman McGrath

Where in New York can you ask a friend to "meet me by the birdcage" and not be referring to the Bronx Zoo? Why the Hotel Inter-Continental New York, of course! Known as The Barclay from its inception in 1926 until acquired by Inter-Continental Hotels in 1978, the birdcage in its lobby has become famous as a meeting point for guests and non-guests alike.

The original concept for The Barclay Hotel was to offer both hotel and residential accommodations to New York's elite. A neo-Federal style was chosen by W & J Sloane, the original designer, to reflect the class and refinement of its potential guests. American Colonial furnishings and murals were in abundance. Patriotic elements such as the American Eagle, stars and liberty cap were incorporated in rug and wall covering designs and ceiling ornamentations.

Early advertisements for The Barclay carried a Colonial motif and described the hotel's philosophy and interiors - "the apartments now leasing revive the traditions of our earliest and most gracious period—The Colonial. Authentic Early American appointments spell comfort and home...gay chintz, old prints, quaint screens, Phyfe and Chippendale furniture, Lowestoft china—Americana of the gracious age."

The hotel opened without fanfare on November 4, 1926, offering 861 rooms, 505 of which were furnished for hotel guests and the remainder for permanent residents who would supply their own furnishings.

By 1933, when the bottom fell out of the economy, two-thirds of New York's hotels found themselves filing for bankruptcy. The Barclay, however, remained solvent. Adjustments had to be made and services were downscaled. However, the economy continued to worsen and in 1937 The Barclay had no choice but to file also.

The '40s saw a toned down resurgence of The Barclay. Rooms were filled to capacity—but largely due to servicemen who dined for free during major holiday seasons. It was during this time that the infamous "birdcage" was constructed in the hotel's lobby under the Tiffany skylight.

As the '50s and '60s approached, The Barclay lost stature. Hotels offering conference facilities and meeting rooms were springing up all over Manhattan. Full-service properties became the order of the day. Mismanagement brought a further decline. By the time Inter-Continental Hotels Corp. (IHC) purchased her in 1978, she was but a shadow of her former self.

Known for their ability to turn around decaying grande dames, Inter-Continental was determined to restore the hotel's decor and dignity. A massive four-year renovation and restoration program was begun at The Barclay. From the kitchens to the guestrooms, no corner was left untouched. Business travelers now take advantage of the newly constructed boardrooms on the third floor.

The homey character, which had eluded The Barclay in the last years, was regained with fine leather sofas, wool carpeting, Oriental screens, Chinoiserie lamps and vases of fresh flowers. Even the original birdcage was replaced at the cost of U.S. $150,000. Exotic birds now inhabit the latticed bronze aviary.

Award-winning guestrooms were painstakingly refurbished by Joseph Grusczak of Joseph Grusczak Associates. Upholstered fruitwood headboards display the hotel's crest, while elegant cherry wood armoires and comfortably upholstered club chairs add to the traditional design.

The dignified spirit of The Barclay has returned to the Hotel Inter-Continental New York.

Lobby (before).

A new latticed bronze birdcage is still the focal point of the lobby (after).

A baby grand piano adds a touch of grace and refinement to the parlor of the Presidential Suite (after).

The luxurious master
bathroom of the
Presidential Suite features
a double jacuzzi (after) .

A lithograph depicting a landscape of upstate New York is given a framed focus by the headboard of the king-size bed (after).

Color tones of blue and warm apricot create a relaxing atmosphere in the sitting area of the Director Suite (after).

Miami Sheraton Bayside At Brickell Point

Miami, Florida USA

Project location
Miami, Florida USA

Hotel company
Interstate Hotels Corp. (operator); Massachusetts Mutual Life Insurance Co. (owner)

Interior design
VHA Incorporated—Carl Newmark; Gloria Diercks; Cheryl Burk

Architecture
VHA Incorporated

Furniture
Albert Martin; Kreiss (*Travertine tables*); **Tropical** (*seating*)

Floor covering
Tai Ping Carpets Ltd. (*area rugs*); **Design Weave**

Photography
Karl Francetic

Miami—Florida's largest city and reputed hub of tourists, sunshine, palm trees and tropical Atlantic beaches, is also a mecca of the hotel industry. Seemingly unending rows of hotels tempt sunsoaked guests into their sultry interiors for a welcome respite.

From the days of its earliest 16th century Spanish explorers to the massive influx of Cubans, Mexicans and South Americans during the 1960s and '70s, a distinctly Spanish character has always influenced the area. It is this theme, flavored with a Caribbean accent, that permeates the Sheraton Bayside at Brickell Point.

The existing hotel did not hold a significant historical posture but was well positioned geographically and the new owners recognized its potential value. Designers at VHA, Inc. of Denver, Colorado, were commissioned to upgrade the design concept and materials to Sheraton standards.

Several factors influenced the eventual design concept—climate, the general condition of the property, the original plan and layout of the hotel, and the area where the hotel was located. Due to a high humidity factor, the existing air-conditioning system was found to be inadequate. To remedy the situation, an additional 50-ton capacity unit was installed. Awnings and fans were added to the exterior lounge terrace to provide guests with relief from the sun and weather. It was for this same reason that the design team decided to add draperies and wooden blinds to all dining room windows.

To promote a tropical feeling throughout the hotel, tones of peach and melon green were selected for both the suites and public areas. Natural wood furnishings, abundant plants and fresh flowers added a Caribbean flair to the hotel.

The original entertainment lounge, which had previously opened into the lobby, was closed in by a combination of wall and glass to reduce noise and improve the effectiveness of the air-conditioning. A complete sound and light system was added to lend focus to the Latin-style entertainment.

A lighting upgrade also played an important role in the renovation. Decorative fixtures were added to public spaces, guestrooms, pre-function areas and ballroom. To improve exterior illumination, new marquee lighting added brightness to the porte cochere to enhance the building's image and create a sense of arrival. In addition, improved lighting of the long, dark driveway provided a safer, better lit environment for both patrons and employees.

With the renovation of the Sheraton Bayside, another jewel has been added to the crown of hotels which encircles Miami.

Accents of red in the floor vases and fresh flowers add focus to the lobby (after).

Registration area (before).

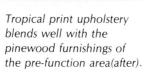

*Tropical print upholstery
blends well with the
pinewood furnishings of
the pre-function area(after).*

Pre-function area (before)

Shell - sculptured chairs convey the tropical theme in the sitting area of a typical suite (after).

Typical suite (before).

Miami Sheraton Bayside at Brickell Point **117**

Bar area in entertainment
lounge (before).

Picture windows
surrounding the
entertainment lounge
promote an outdoor
atmosphere. Floral
carpeting adds a colorful
accent to the bar (after).

The New World Hotel

Kowloon, Kong Kong

Project location
Hong Kong

Hotel company
New World Hotels International, Ltd.

Interior design
Gauer Design Far East, Ltd.—Jane Arnett/*Director*

Lighting
First Collections

Wall covering
St. John Bosco Trust Co.

Floor covering
Carpet Gallery

Photography
Joseph Sy

Tsim Sha Tsui, a popular shopping and business district in Hong Kong, promotes keen competition amongst hotels located in the area. Consequently, renovation is an ongoing process from which most are not immune. It can either involve the entire hotel or emphasize individual areas that require updating.

In the case of The New World Hotel, focus was placed on converting its outdated top European eating establishment into a high class Chinese restaurant. The management felt the time was ripe for a new image rather than updating that which already existed. It was evident that only a complete redesign of the facility would accomplish this.

According to Jane Arnett, the director of Gauer Design Far East Ltd., "The design concept was to incorporate a garden theme into the interior by implementing various elements from a typical Chinese garden pavillion or tea house. It was also our aim to mesh contemporary Chinese pieces and details with more traditional ones."

One of the obstacles encountered by the design team was an overall low ceiling height. They were able to achieve small increases by sculpturing around air-conditioning ductwork and drainage pipes. Moulding and illumination added to the visual effect.

A new covered walkway entrance, paved with detailed patterns of a traditional Chinese garden, leads guests into the dining area. Custom-designed timber lattice screens frame the view over the surrounding foliage.

The large open areas of the restaurant were subdivided by timber screens and Oriental artwork. A contemporary Chinese design was selected for the chairs. Ms. Arnett adds, "The color scheme of red, green and black was influenced by the colors found in a Mandarin's robe and intended to blend the overall Chinese theme."

Wall panels are accented with mirrors and modern light fixtures. The lattice pattern of the timber screens is also repeated in the carpet design. Lighting is generally subdued with halogen lamps highlighting tables and artwork.

Ms. Arnett concludes, "Views to the gardens and planting areas, which are spotlit at night, help to create an unusual and successful restaurant popular both with hotel guests and Hong Kong residents."

Entrance to former Park Lane Restaurant (before).

*Old Chinese artifacts
welcome guests entering
the new Dynasty
Restaurant (after).*

The New World Hotel **121**

The covered walkway entrance was introduced from the garden area with views framed by timber lattice screens (after).

(before).

The large open area of the restaurant is subdivided by timber screens and Chinese artwork and the chairs are of a contemporary Chinese design (after).

The Omni Hong Kong

Hong Kong

Project location
Hong Kong

Hotel company
Omni Hotels Asia Pacific

Interior design
Gauer Design Far East Ltd.—Marianne Gauer/*Managing Director;*
Jane Arnett/*Director;* **Thomas Wan/***Project Manager;* **Grace Chu/**
Project Coordinator

Lighting
Richardo Lighting Co. Ltd.; First Collections

Furniture
Kuen Lee Decoration & Furniture Co. Ltd.

Wall covering
St. John Bosco Trust Co.

Floor covering
Carpet World; Carpet Gallery

Photography
Joseph Sy

It was the third time around for the group at Gauer
Design Far East Ltd. Each of the two previous renovations
of the Omni HongKong Hotel, in 1979 and 1982, had
been directed by them and in 1987 they were given
another opportunity to leave their mark. This time the
project entailed the conversion of two of the nine
guestroom levels into "executive" floors.

It was important that a theme be selected which would
distinguish the new area from the remainder of the
property. The concept proposed by the designers was
an ambience reminiscent of a sophisticated,
elegant European hotel. Asian artwork and artifacts
would add an Oriental touch to reinforce the traditional
culture of the local region.

A total of 120 rooms, elevator lobbies and corridors
underwent a complete redesign and renovation. An
Executive Lounge was added for the convenience and
comfort of the "executive" guests.

Upon arrival, guests are welcomed into a club-like
atmosphere created by the extensive use of maplewood
paneling throughout. Jane Arnett, the director of Gauer
Design, notes, "The wood panel theme was continued
into the suites but was detailed differently and stained a
gold color to contrast with the more subdued maple
used elsewhere." All furnishings, which were exclusively
designed for the two executive floors, are characterized
by a distinct Biedermeier influence. Gold and black,
colors often associated with strength and power, were
chosen to reinforce the atmosphere of stately grandeur.

Rosa Amora marble floors and walls, accented wth
granite borders and countertop, convey the essence of
luxury in the new bathrooms. Shower cubicles, of
exquisitely etched tempered glass, complete the refined,
high style effect.

Mirrored niches in the wood paneled corridors and
elevator lobbies highlight a variety of Asian artifacts.
Handpainted silk murals on the walls of the hallways
guide guests on the way to their suites.

Ms. Arnett concludes, "The final product reflects the
standards of elegance expected by the business executive
who seeks the service and comfort of a top class hotel
while away from home."

Elevator lobby (before).

Large handpainted silk wall
murals perk up the wood
panelled elevator lobby (after).

Bedroom of typical suite (before).

New recessed lighting and light-colored carpeting and wall treatment brighten up the bedroom area of the typical suite (after).

Black detailing of custom-
designed furniture provides
a handsome contrast to the
natural wood dining chairs (after).

Sitting room of typical
suite (before)

Granite borders and
countertop enhance the
Rosa Amora marble
surroundings of the
bathroom (after).

Bathroom (before).

Corridor (before).

Mirrored niches are spotlit to emphasize Asian artwork in the maplewood paneled corridors (after).

The Peninsula New York

New York, New York USA

Project location
New York, New York USA

Hotel company
Pratt Hotel Company

Interior design
Hirsch/Bedner and Associates—Howard Hirsch, Sandra Cortner-Dunn

Architecture
AI Group Architects

Lighting
JDA New York (consultant); **Louis Baldinger & Sons** (custom)

Furniture
Drexel, Bibi International (guestroom casepieces)

Floor covering
Crowthers, England (public area carpets); **Tai Ping** (handmade area carpets)

Photography
Jaime Ardilles-Arce

In the corner of 5th Avenue and 55th Street, an address easily remembered, stands The Peninsula New York—a hotel not easily forgotten. Purchased by the Peninsula Group of Hong Kong in October 1988, the once destitute hotel has again joined the ranks of luxury accommodations in Manhattan.

Designed in 1902 by architects Hiss and Weekes, and completed in 1905, the former Gotham Hotel was meant to reflect a residential character and operate as an apartment hotel. Its Beaux Arts style, accompanied by Italian Renaissance detailing, was chosen to blend in with the architecture of its surroundings. Indeed, while under construction in 1902, the hotel was singled out by Architectural Record as one of the first buildings to harmonize with its environs.

The lobby, undersized by today's standards, was designed to be adequate for the hotel guests, yet small enough to discourage loungers. Every suite had a butler's pantry, served with a heated dumbwaiter. Each of the 400 guestrooms boasted a bath. Potted plants and a domed ceiling of leaded glass characterized the Palm Room, the only area in the hotel where smoking was permitted at all hours. (An interesting restriction for the turn of the century.) In the adjacent "writing room," private cabinets were available for making telephone calls and sending telegrams.

During The Gotham's first renovation in 1939, guestrooms were reduced to 321. A second renovation was attempted in 1979 by Rene Hatt, a Swiss color psychologist and hotel developer. The project was well underway when Hatt ran out of funds and bankruptcy resulted in the closure of The Gotham for seven years. In the mid '80s, The Pratt Corporation acquired the property. After a two-year rejuvenation program, the old grand lady was reopened in the spring of 1988 as Maxim's de Paris. Several months later, realizing the

value and choice location of the landmark building, the Peninsula Group purchased the newly remodeled hotel.

The design team from Hirsch/Bedner & Associates was instrumental in resurrecting the charm and elegance once synonymous with The Gotham. From the original Cherbonnier armoire in the lobby to the replicated headboards in the bedrooms, a late 19th century Art Nouveau decor permeates the hotel's interiors. Many of the antique pieces, from such masters as Louis Majorelle, Eugene Gaillard and Emile Galle, were personally selected by Howard Hirsch during his travels throughout Europe.

Upon entering the lobby, a sweeping staircase—constructed of rich Bianco Classico marble imported from Italy—guides guests to the reception area on the mezzanine level. The decidedly French decor also adorns the hotel's two restaurants, Le Bistro and Adrienne. Original prints by Alphons Mucha, a Hungarian artist famous for his poster art, grace the elegant eatery's walls as do photos of Sarah Bernhardt.

A glass-enclosed fitness center, steeped in rich wood paneling and plush carpeting, was carved out of the top three floors of the 23-story building. It offers its members state-of-the-art exercise facilities and a roof-top view of New York's spectacular skyline.

Without doubt, Hirsch/Bedner's sensitive attention to architectural style and historical detail has recreated the former spirit and splendor of a once grand hotel.

Art Nouveau furnishings offer refinement to the registration and concierge desk area (after).

The added height of a
cathedral ceiling promotes
an airy, outdoor feeling in
the elevator lobby(after).

Hand-painted wall murals
add interest and color to
the decor of the Gotham
Lounge (after).

Regal grandeur abounds in the master bedroom of the Presidential Suite (after).

Belle Epoque sconces and the soft hues of salmon-pink walls reinforce the characteristically French influence in the design of the Adrienne Restaurant (after).

A view into the second bedroom from the sitting room of the Presidential Suite (after).

Pflaum's Posthotel Pegnitz

Pegnitz, West Germany

Project location
Pegnitz, West Germany

Hotel company
Andreas Pflaum

Interior Design
Dirk Obliers Design—Friedholm Hubner

Lighting
Dirk Obliers Design

Wall covering
Tescoha

Photography
Dirk Obliers Design

One of the most exciting and unusual luxury suites in the hotel world can be found at the Pflaum's Posthotel Pegnitz. To stay there is to be transported through a surrealistic odyssey from which you may not wish to return.

This very unconventional suite, the "Venus in Blue," was the brainchild of a very unconventional man, Dirk Obliers, president of Dirk Obliers Design GmbH of West Germany. Not one to dabble in traditionalism, Obliers feels that the future of luxury accommodations lies not, as he says, in the "exorbitant accumulation of ostentatious materials," but rather in "a designer's courage to be creative and innovative."

Obliers explains, "The mere collecting and arranging of modern furniture is without any doubt the wrong incentive to arouse the guest's interest in modern design conceptions." He and his design team look upon themselves as conceptual visionaries rather than conventional interior designers.

It is with this philosophy that Obliers approached the challenge of renovating the 300-year-old posthouse-inn. Owned by a famous pair of eccentric culinary brothers, Andreas and Hermann Pflaum, the hotel is located in the heart of West Germany's Bayreuth Festival country. According to Obliers, "The design team's aim was to meld function and adventure while employing good design solutions and unusual combinations of materials."

A bedroom/bathroom ensemble—a high-tech four-poster bed and a whirlpool bath—comprise the center of the suite. Here, guests find the comfort and spirit of a modern oasis. By using a modern light fiber technique, a twinkling starry sky is reproduced, reminiscent of the stars in the Northern sky. Quadrophonic sound, integrated with the starry visual effect, creates a soothing ambience. The whirlpool, set in a base of colored kaolin sand and real tent cloth, completes the picture of an oasis—sand, water, tent and a clear starlit sky.

Some of the design requirements could not be met by items available on the market. "Fixtures such as large sconces, bathroom lamps, washstands, side tables, cabinet towers, the minibar and hi-fi pedestals, were specially designed and exclusively produced for us," adds Obliers. However, he notes, "Exclusivity and luxury of materials was not guided by a generous investment budget but rather by the combination of innovative ideas and their respective realization."

An evening spent in the "Venus in Blue" suite of the Pflaum's Posthotel Pegnitz can be the "conversation piece" of a lifetime—which is exactly what Dirk Obliers intended it to be.

Bedroom/sitting room area before renovation.

Geometric lighting fixtures flank the entry into the bedroom/bathroom area of the "Venus in Blue" suite (after).

Varying shades of blue and white in the cabinet design provide a handsome contrast while framing whirlpool area (after).

A skylight provides
additional light to the attic
sitting room (after).

Sitting room before
renovation.

The multi-colored kaolin sand base of the whirlpool adds to the suite's aura of a modern oasis *(after)*.

A view from the bed to the sitting room *(after)*.

Mirrors and varied custom-designed lighting add interest to a very contemporary but functional bathroom (after).

A swivel stand TV entertains guests while they relax in bed or in the whirlpool (after).

Modern comfort is
provided by two
upholstered chairs in the
sitting room (after).

Quinta Real

Zacatecas, Mexico

Project location
Zacatecas, Mexico

Hotel company
Quinta Real Zacatecas S.A.

Interior design
Elias & Elias—Richard Elias; Robert Elias

Architecture
Elias & Elias

Photography
No credit given

Today's hoteliers acknowledge that comfort and service do not always insure a guest's return visit to their property. Often, added amenities or an atmosphere, created by an unusual design, can make the difference. In the case of the Quinta Real Zacatecas, the latter is sufficient guarantee for a return. For how often does one get the opportunity to stay in a 300-year-old bullring?

This is a project in which restoration, renovation and preservation all played an equally important role. The 18th century bullring of San Pedro, thought to be the second oldest on the North American continent, had been declared a national monument. Its deteriorated condition, however, prevented further use as a bullfight arena.

Elias & Elias, a Mexican architectural/interior design firm located in Guadalajara, was retained by the proprietors of the landmark to develop a design concept which would assimilate the existing historic remains of the arena into the modern concept of hospitality lodging. This was not an easy task. According to Richard Elias, "Adapting the functions of a hotel into the existing circular construction of the bullring presented difficulties. Also, a new foundation had to be laid to support the use of the upper portion of the ring." Careful research and in-depth analysis of various alternatives resulted in the creation of a new building which appears to be a natural extension of the old historic structure.

To enter the 50-room hotel, one must pass under the arches of the city's ancient stone aqueduct—a landmark itself—which partially surrounds the property. Once inside, the traditional charm of Mexican culture is more than evident. Regional artifacts contribute color and interest to the public spaces. The restaurant, which has been mounted on the bullring's original "graderia," or seats, offers dining on several levels.

Due to the multi-planed, circular configuration of the building, guestrooms vary in shape and size, depending on the area of the ring in which they were built. Walls of brick and stone add a rustic touch to the rooms, and bronze fixtures handsomely accent the marble bathroom interiors.

One of the most delightful aspects of the Quinta Real is the Bar, cozily nestled under the seats of the bullring. Sitting beneath the original arches (which were intentionally left untouched), patrons can envision the excitement of the matadors and cheering crowds which once dominated the historic arena. Only fireplaces were added to complete the setting.

Unlike the bulls that passed but once through the bullring of San Pedro, guests return continually to enjoy the treasures of Zacatecas and to relive history through the architectural wonder it spawned.

View from the bullring (before).

Hotel entrance through the arches of the ancient stone aqueduct of the city of Zacatecas (after).

*Aerial view of the Quinta
Real (after).*

*Exterior view of the lobby
from the bullring (after).*

"The Arena" was changed
to a plaza for open events
with a design using stone,
cantera and grass (after).

*Interior view of old
bullring of San Pedro with
adjacent aqueduct (before).*

*The restaurant was
mounted on the
"graderia" (seats) of the
bullring (after).*

*Arched entrance to the
inside guestroom patio (after).*

Walls of brick and stone add rustic appeal to typical bedroom (after).

Bronze fixtures handsomely accent marbled bathroom interior (after).

*Fireplaces and bright-
colored furnishings perk up
the arched surroundings of
the Bar, located beneath
the seats of the bullring (after).*

Traditional Mexican decor and hospitality greet diners in the multi-leveled restaurant (after).

Radisson Normandie Hotel

San Juan, Puerto Rico

Project location
San Juan, Puerto Rico

Hotel company
Normandie Limited Partnership, S.E.

Interior design
C.S.A., Inc.—Herman Crawford; Domingo J. Galan Associates

Architecture
Domingo J. Galan Associates

Photography
Clay Humphries

If ocean liners can be referred to as sailing hotels, reverse logic would appropriately describe the Radisson Normandie Hotel as a land-bound cruise ship. Legend has it that Felix Benitez Rexach, a wealthy local businessman and engineer, had the hotel build in 1939 for his French wife, Moineau. The hotel was designed to replicate the famous SS Normandie, on which the Rexachs often sailed to and from Europe. Indeed, they were said to have honeymooned on the vessel.

Raul G. Reichard, the architect solicited by Rexach to oversee the project, held a fondness for the Art Deco style of architecture. His blending of such neoclassical elements as Egyptian, Roman and French motifs found in columns and window treatments created a flamboyant yet elegant design. Dominican wood stairways led patrons to their rooms where colonial-style beds of mahogany wood awaited them. High ceilings and open balconies in the guestrooms promoted fresh air circulation.

The demise of the Normandie began in the late 1950s. As Felix Benitez Rexach paid less attention to the property (spending less time there following his wife's death), new modern hotels began springing up around the Normandie, cutting into her popularity and profit. A lack of air-conditioning and a decline in services and maintenance led to its closure in July 1976.

After a long, hard-fought battle by city preservationists, the "pride of Puerto Rico" was declared a Historical Monument on August 29, 1980. Upon acquisition by the Normandie Limited Partnership in July 1987, the hotel was franchised to the Radisson Hotel Corp. and subsequently underwent a U.S. $20 million restoration and renovation program.

The once-alluring Art Deco interiors were recreated through the efforts of two design teams working closely together—CSA, Inc. of Minneapolis and Domingo J. Galan Associates of Puerto Rico. It was important that the integrity of the original design be retained as much as possible. Consequently, the ceiling heights and spaciousness of the 180 guestrooms were maintained, despite the installation of a new air-conditioning system. Guests can now reach their floors while enjoying a panoramic view of the hotel's interior, via two glass-enclosed elevators which glide along the sides of the plexiglass-domed atrium.

Finding skilled craftsmen for a restoration project can often present a challenge to the design team. In the case of the Radisson Normandie, luck prevailed when the son of the artisan who did the property's original plasterwork was located to recreate his father's artistic craftsmanship.

Unlike many of the grand hotels in Puerto Rico, the Radisson Normandie does not offer a casino to its patrons—a factor that contributed to its earlier failure. Management's decision to promote a quietly elegant atmosphere of relaxation, in a nautical setting away from the tumult of gambling facilities at adjacent hotels, has met with overwhelming guest approval. Patrons again enjoy the pleasures of a Caribbean cruise without ever leaving land.

Aerial view of exterior (before).

Exterior view shows the recently added outdoor pool (after).

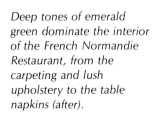

A scalloped indirect
lighting fixture adds an Art
Deco touch to the Front
Desk area (after).

Deep tones of emerald
green dominate the interior
of the French Normandie
Restaurant, from the
carpeting and lush
upholstery to the table
napkins (after).

A lavender and blue color scheme, reminiscent of soothing Caribbean waters, is characteristic of most guestrooms and the Club Normandie Executive Lounge (after).

Plasterwork of the Gold Room ceiling was recreated by the son of the original artisan (after).

Ramada Downtown

Tucson, Arizona USA

Project location
Tucson, Arizona USA

Interior design
Design Trend International Interiors, Ltd. —Robert Algiere, Louise Corbitt, David Wharton

Lighting
Scottsdale Lighting

Furniture
Design Marketing (*chairs*); **Tivoli Fountain** (*fountain*)

Floor covering
Darkan (*carpet*); **Mexican Tile Co.** (*decorative tile*)

Photography
Mark Boisclair

Set against the backdrop of the spectacular Santa Catalina, Tucson and Rincon mountain ranges of Tucson, Arizona, stands the newly renovated Ramada Downtown Hotel. Even though the 30-year-old property continued to attract patrons, it was clear that a long overdue upgrading of its facilities was necessary to maintain its popularity.

When Robert Algiere, president of Design Trend International Interiors, Inc., was approached to redesign the property in 1985, he was faced with the problem of "transforming the existing architecture and interior space planning from a Southern Georgian Colonial design to a Southwestern Territorial motif. It was our opinion that the architecture in this area should reflect the characteristic flavor of the region," he says.

To accomplish this, the design team disguised the old hip roof by building facade walls of varying heights to create a wallscape resembling the style of a Southwestern building ensemble. A Spanish flair was added to the exterior by using wrought iron detailing for balconies, window implants with lace curtains and hand-formed saltillo clay roofing tiles imported from Mexico. Algiere adds, "Fountains were positioned around the entrance to create a Mexican territorial atmosphere as could be found around a hacienda."

Renovating the hotel's interior also presented a challenge. It was originally designed with an oversized convention reception lobby which had to be reduced to eliminate congestion and provide intimacy. The front desk was relocated closer to the entrance door and a separate convention guest check-in area added. The space surrounding the existing circular staircase was expanded with the construction of a pass-through underneath. This permitted access into the "food court."

To continue the Southwestern motif into the interiors, saltillo roof tiles were used on the main port cochere and entryway and continued into the interior spaces on the roof eyebrows. Wrought iron detailing on interior balconies added to an indoor street scene. Four skylights cut into the roof line allow natural light to filter through for the abundant foliage growing within.

A new restaurant bakery provides full-breakfast service and a take-out window which faces the lobby, for on-the-go guests wanting a quick coffee and croissant.

To best exploit the mountain view, the hotel's lounge was relocated to the west end of the building and expanded onto the patio. With the addition of an island bar (featuring a cascading waterfall), guests can now relax in a Mexican-inspired tropical atmosphere.

Creative attention was also paid to the guestrooms. Algiere explains, "We elected to continue the Southwestern ambience by introducing a soft color palette of peaches, corals and teals into the rooms by using custom-printed bedspreads and artwork. Casegoods were finished in a very light natural washed look with regional artifacts completing the look."

The outstanding redesign of the Ramada Downtown was recognized in 1987 with the "Renovation of the Year" award from the Ramada Hotel Corporation.

A Southwestern look was created for the front desk with saltillo roof tiles and soft curving arches (after).

Front desk (before).

The circular staircase remains the focal point of the lobby. Foliage and Spanish-style fountain add a Southwestern flair (after).

Lobby (before).

Lobby interior (before).

Intimacy is created in the
street-like lobby with the
addition of meeting spots,
gift shops and overhangs (after).

Typical guestroom (before).

A soft color palette of
peaches, corals and teals
are introduced into the
guestroom through custom-
printed bedspreads and
regional artwork (after).

The new bakery offers table and counter dining as well as an express take-out window for guests on-the-go (after).

restaurant (before).

The restaurant was expanded and remodeled from a coffee counter service to a modern dining area (after).

Bar/Lounge (before).

Interior and exterior view
of the newly relocated
lounge (after).

Ramada Hotel Laleli Istanbul

Istanbul, Turkey

Project location
Istanbul, Turkey

Hotel company
Loytas

Interior design
Ertem Ertunga and Mim-Ar—Ertem Ertunga; Perfectra; Cassina

Architecture
Ertem Ertunga Architecture and Urban Planning Office

Lighting
Licht Im Raum; Joachim Dinnebier

Furniture
Cassina

Floor covering
Sezak (*carpets*); **Buchtal** (*ceramic tiles*)

Photography
Tamer Yilmaz

Heading westward on Ordu Street, away from Beyazit Square in the Old City of Istanbul, one encounters the magnificent Ramada Hotel Laleli. The edifice was not previously a hotel, but rather four separate apartment buildings, each four stories high, situated at right angles to each other with open courtyards in the center. Formerly the "Harikzadegan" Apartments, they were the first buildings in the city to be built of concrete. These housed families left homeless by the great fire of Cibali-Fatih-Altinmermer in 1918, which destroyed 7,500 homes.

The four buildings were comprised of 124 apartments and 25 shops. From the 1930s through the 1970s they housed low-income families under a rent-control system which, unfortunately, was not adequate enough to maintain the properties in a habitable condition. Although the structures survived, the interiors deteriorated to a derelict state.

Under the guidance of architect and engineer Ertem Ertunga, a massive restoration and reconstruction program was undertaken in 1986. It lasted 22 months, and transformed the four buildings into a 275-room hotel. According to Mr. Ertunga, "The interior installations and layouts were completely redone without changing the original facade and character of the original structures at all."

The four units were linked together using Lexan, a transparent, insulating, dome-shaped material. This resulted in the formation of a formal entrance, reception area, passageway and various public spaces within the criss-crossed alleys between the buildings. Ertunga continues, "The open courtyards were also covered by this material to enable functional utilization of interior spaces such as restaurants and lounges."

Attics, which were once used for laundry, were converted into luxury studios with slanted ceilings and attractive layouts.

As with any transformation of this magnitude, problems arose. Ertunga explains, "By far the most difficult part of the conversion process involved the procurement of sufficient space in the hotel to house such utilities as the kitchen, heating system and power units. We were forced to excavate almost two levels below the foundation to provide the necessary space."

Floor layouts were completely redesigned, dividing larger apartments into individual guestrooms. Among the amenities incorporated into the new hotel were three restaurants, a bar, two lobbies, a casino, a pool, fitness center, conference and banquet rooms, a snack bar and pastry shop.

Exterior view of apartment buildings before conversion into hotel (before).

Courtyard was enclosed
using Lexan to form a
domed ceiling (after).

Inner courtyard (before).

Guests can choose to dine
in quiet seclusion inside
the restaurant (after).

Surrounding walkways provide guests with a good view of the Dynasty Restaurant located on the main level of the domed atrium (after).

Exterior view of courtyard before conversion into the Dynasty Restaurant (before).

A sleek contemporary look characterizes the new Babali Bar.

Interior of bar area before conversion.

Rambagh Palace Hotel

Jaipur, India

Project location
Jaipur, India

Interior design
Taj Group of Hotels

Interior design
Taj Group of Hotels, The Indian Hotels Co. Ltd.; Taj Mahal Hotel, Apollo Bunder, Bombay (In-house)—Elizabeth Kerkar

Architecture
Taj Group of Hotels

Photography
D.L. Oberoi; Robin Morrison

Maharani Suite sitting room (before).

"P" alace" hotels represent some of the most luxurious properties found in the international hotel industry. They are 5-star grande dames with an added touch of monarchial distinction which places them a notch above the rest. Within this same category, however, a differentiation exists. A "true" palace hotel usually once housed a ruling royal family, and in some cases, still does. The others, even though they may boast a proud and varied history, were built as lodging establishments for the public, albeit wealthy public, while emulating the "real" thing.

The Rambagh Palace was built in 1835 as a four-room pavillion for Maharaja Sawai Ram Singh II, who ruled the House of Amber (Jaipur) from 1835 to 1880. Legend notes that it was named Kesar Badaran's Bagh, after Ram Singh's governess and his mother's favorite badaran (handmaiden), Kesar. The bounty of big game found in the woodlands surrounding Jaipur, made it a favorite hunting lodge for the royal family and remained so during Ram Singh's reign. To accommodate visiting royal guests, several rooms were added in 1887, and the adjoining natural wilderness was transformed into lush sculptured gardens. It was during this period that the structure became known as the Rambagh.

For a time, the 26-room mansion served as a private school for Prince Man Singh. As he took over the reigns of power, Rambagh was declared his official residence and was elevated to the status of a Palace in 1925. As the ruling families of India gradually lost their power and imperial posture, all efforts were made by Man Singh to save the royal family's residence from extinction. The painful decision to convert the property into a hotel was made in 1957. Some of Man Singh's fellow Maharajas were disgruntled, struggling to come to terms with their vanishing lifestyle. However, many of them soon followed suit, converting their own properties to hotels. When the Taj Group of Hotels took over the management of the Rambagh Palace in 1971, a decision was made to renovate the property while restoring the elegance and original splendor of its craftsmanship. Facilities were updated to conform with today's hospitality needs and requirements.

The project's major obstacle was the thickness of the original stone walls. These were practically impenetrable with drills, and had to be hand-chiselled to permit installation of air-conditioning ducts. To camouflage grills and smoke detectors, decorative mouldings and cornices blended them into the ceiling design. Windows were carefully glazed so that the original architectural elements of the building were not spoiled.

One century and 110 rooms later, the Rambagh Palace Hotel stands as a testament to the pampered luxury of royal life—one which can now be savored by all!

One of the most imperial guestrooms of the palace is the Pothikhana. A royal burgundy color scheme blends smartly with the surrounding wood paneling (after).

(before).

Maharani Suite bedroom (before).

Cream-colored sofas
provide an appealing
contrast to the earthtone
surroundings of the
bedroom (after).

Maharaja Suite bedroom (before).

The fabric used for the
bedspread is repeated in
the headboard and
overhead valance of the
regal bedroom (after).

From the sitting room of the Princess Suite, large arched windows provide an appealing view of the surrounding gardens (after).

The Sagamore Hotel Resort and Conference Center

Sagamore Island, Bolton Landing, New York USA

Project location
Sagamore Island, Bolton Landing, New York USA

Hotel company
Green Island Associates

Interior design
Daroff Design Inc.—Karen Daroff/*Principal-in-Charge*; **John D. Borne**/*Project Manager*; **Thomas McHugh**/*Senior Designer*

Architecture
Alesker Reiff & Dundon Inc.—Bill Alesker

Lighting
Lighting Design Collaborative (consultant); Chapman (*lobby, Trillium Pre-Assembly, Country Queen bedroom, Adirondack bedroom*); **Virginia Metalcrafters** (*Trillium, dining room*); **Stephen Gerould** (*Country Queen bedroom*); **Norman Perry** (*Adirondack bedroom*)

Furniture
Ashley Manor (*lobby, Trillium Pre-Assembly*); **Drexel Heritage** (*lobby, Trillium, bedrooms*); **Wright Table Co.** (*Trillium Pre-Assembly*); **Kittinger** (*lobby, Trillium Pre-Assembly*); **Wood & Hogan** (*Trillium Pre-Assembly*); **L & B Products** (*Trillium, dining room*); **Hickory Chair** (*Trillium Pre-Assembly, Trillium*); **Creations Drucker S.A.** (*dining room*); **Thomasville** (*bedrooms*); **Habersham Plantation** (*bedrooms*); **Zimports** (*bedrooms*); **Shelby Williams** (*Mr. Brown's Cafe*); **Robert Doyle** (*Mr. Brown's Cafe*); **Cedarquist** (*Mr. Brown's Cafe*)

Wall covering
B.F. Goodrich (*dining room*)

Floor covering
Edward Molina (*Trillium, dining room*); **Harbinger** (*Country Queen bedroom*)

Photography
Paul Warchol

Located on a 72-acre island, the original complex of buildings now known as The Sagamore served as a social center and guest house for five prominent Philadelphia families who summered each year at Lake George in upstate New York. The main house, an X-shaped three-story structure, was built in 1883 to provide rooms for guests and staff. The five families resided in the nearby cottages. The complex also included outbuildings, a carriage house and stables, an 88-acre golf course (on the nearby mainland), and various berths for yachts and small craft. Declared a historical landmark, the main house was converted into a summer hotel in 1929 and a swimming pool was added in the 1930s.

To the design group at Daroff Design Inc. in Philadelphia, restoring the historic property presented a special design opportunity. They were employed to create a theme and mood which would encompass the hotel and the entire 72-acre island environment as well. "We chose to combine an historic 'turn-of-the-century' motif with Adirondack and rustic country-style detailing to evoke the original spirit of this 1883 Victorian summer resort," explains the firm's president, Karen Daroff.

Working with developer Norman Wolgin and the Green Island Associates, the design team completed the restoration and renovation in 26 months. While the exterior was restored to its original Victorian splendor, the interiors were carefully crafted to suggest 19th century charm. Ms. Daroff adds, "The only major alteration to the existing hotel structure was the enclosure of the portico to serve as the 'high tea' focal point of the facility while accommodating year-round use."

The main building was restored with 100 guestrooms and suites done in American Country, Neo-Colonial and Adirondack styles. In addition, 250 new cottages were constructed and designed in a rustic country decor.

Challenges to the design team were many, not the least of which was meeting preservation requirements. Superfluous structures that did not conform to the main house's style were removed. The materials from these buildings were then used to replace and reinforce the main house's facade. The interior, however, required total gutting.

New plumbing, heating and air-conditioning systems had to be installed without damaging the building's historic character. According to Ms. Daroff, "We wished to preserve and maintain as much of the original millwork and detailing as possible. The solution involved dismantling the entire building, mapping and storing the pieces and locating covert spaces behind walls and pillar covers for each wire, convector and pipe." Key elements were then restored, reassembled and incorporated back into the design of the interiors. Each item of historical merit was saved, refurbished or recycled.

"The existing lobby was deemed too narrow and confining to accommodate the hotel's registration function. So we added a separate reception-arrival building to the original entry-drive. The new pavilion has a strong design affinity with the existing house and removes the hustle and bustle of the arrival and departure from the main building," notes Daroff. In a return to its former quiet elegance, the lobby offers a subdued, "living-room" atmosphere in which to relax.

From the moment guests arrive on the island, they are whisked away into a fantasy of Old World charm. Every detail reflects the grace and romance of this historic era.

Exterior (before).

Exterior (after) .

Lobby (before) .

Comfortable period furnishings add an elegant charm to the lobby (after) .

Undulating leather-upholstered partitions insure privacy in Mr. Brown's Cafe (after).

Mr. Brown's Cafe (before).

The Trillium Restaurant (before).

Majestic fluted columns dominate the environs of the Trillium Restaurant (after).

Dining Room (before).

Diners enjoy the view of Lake George and its surroundings from the windows of the country-style dining room (after).

Private guestroom (before)

Rustic decor permeates the Adirondack Bedroom (after).

Entry into the Wine Cellar from the Trillium Pre-assembly Room (after).

A pinewood four-poster bed enhances the colonial atmosphere of the Country Queen Bedroom (after).

The Sheraton Carlton

Washington, DC

Project location
Washington, D.C. USA

Hotel company
The Sheraton Corp.

Interior design
Hochheiser—Elias Design Group, Inc.—Brad Elias, Jacques Jacquet, Alice Cottrell

Architecture
Segreti-Tepper Architects

Lighting
C.M. Kling & Associates (*lobby, exterior*); **Coronet** (*guestroom, suite*); **Royal Haeger** (*guestroom*); **Paul Hanson** (*guestroom, suite*); **Remington** (*guestroom, suite*)

Furniture
Kimball Hospitality Furniture (*guestroom, suite*); **Style Rite Furniture** (*guestroom, suite*); **Baker** (*suite, lobby*); **Drexel** (*suite, lobby*); **Bernhardt** (*suite*); **Kay Lynn** (*lobby*); **DIA** (*lobby*); **Shelby Williams** (*restaurant*)

Wall covering
Sellers & Johnson (*guestroom*); **Kinny** (*suite*); **Schumacher** (*suite*)

Floor covering
Shaw Industries (*guestroom, suite*); **Couristan** (*suite*); **Thai Rugs** (*lobby*); **Harbinger** (*restaurant*); **Hugh McKay** (*corridor, public areas*)

Photography
Clay Humphries

Some say that Washington, DC—the capital of the United States, and the political center of the world—lacks for little. Stately government buildings, celebrated monuments and renowned politicians are all in abundance. Almost as numerous are the hotels spread along its avenues and streets. Although tradition and elegance are expected, only a handful of these lodging establishments stand in a class of their own—one of refined graciousness and luxurious dignity.

The Sheraton Carlton is a prime example. Conceived by Harry Wardman, a successful tradesman, the hotel was built in 1926 to house his elite friends. The property was designed by Turkish architect Mirhan Mesrobian, in an Italian Renaissance style characterized by ornate, gold-gilded ceilings, large oval windows and decorative furnishings. Such decor was popular amongst the merchant princes of Venice, Florence and Milan.

As the years went by, The Carlton's unique design was enhanced by the addition of several English and French architectural embellishments. Closed in 1987, the property underwent an extensive U.S. $16 million renovation and restoration process which saw its interiors enriched by a new American Eclectic appearance.

Upon entering the lobby, attention is immediately drawn to the opulent furnishings displayed throughout— including Louis XV Versailles chandeliers, Louis XVI and Italian Rococo sconces, and a ceiling of ornamental plaster with Florentine designed beams. With another glance, one notes the Italian Renaissance Florentine scroll work rug and baroque and French Empire Damask fabric furnishings. In the Crystal Room, draperies of striped Venetian silk accent the 21-foot arched window. And who can miss the original Louis XV Bombe Chest gracing the Chandelier Room?

No area of the hotel was left untouched by the renovation process. Indeed, the superior, detailed craftsmanship exhibited at the Sheraton Carlton merited the 1989 Craftsmanship Award, bestowed by the Washington Building Congress. Its old world charm and ambiance have guaranteed its place as a respected Washington institution.

Lobby (before).

Existing painted ceiling was restored and enhanced by concealed lighting in the beams. Furnishings are American Eclectic (after).

Sitting area of typical suite (before).

A glass-enclosed shower stall is the focal point of the marble-rich bathroom of the Vice Presidential Suite (after).

Overstuffed furnishings enhance the relaxed feel of the redesigned sitting room (after).

The Presidential Suite was
garnered from an existing
suite and three bedrooms.
It is fitted with bulletproof
glass and special security
systems for visiting
dignitaries (after).

The Allegro Restaurant was transformed from a dark hotel eatery to a popular Bistro-style establishment (after).

Restaurant (before).

Ceiling detail in Allegro Restaurant (after).

One of many antique pieces gracing the entrance to the restaurant (after).

St. James's Club

Los Angeles, California USA

Project location
Los Angeles, California USA

Hotel company
St. James's Clubs International/Norfolk Capital Hotels

Interior design
David Becker

Architecture
David Gray & Associates

Photography
Denis Freppel; Tom Bonner

To stay at the St. James's Club on Sunset Boulevard is to relive Hollywood's Golden Age of the '30s and '40s—an era when Art Deco was the style of choice. The Sunset Tower, as it was then called, was designed in 1929 by Leland Bryant, a prominent architect, as a luxury apartment/hotel complex.

It was initially recognized for its unique "earthquake-proof" construction. The building was the first in California to be built on "rockers," rather than on a foundation set in bedrock, and the first to be entirely serviced by electricity. Its smooth gray facade was offset by plaster friezes depicting the "Age of Travel." For many years, such noted personalities as Jean Harlow, Clark Gable, Howard Hughes and Marilyn Monroe considered it "home."

As post-war Hollywood began to lose its luster, the complex fell into disrepair and decay until 1980 when Englishman Peter DeSavary acquired it. To DeSavary, the 1983 and 1991 America's Cup challenger and owner of three other St. James's Clubs (London, Paris, and Antigua), spending U.S. $40 million to restore the Sunset Tower was a wise investment. Its unique Art Deco architectural features contributed to its inclusion, in 1979, to the National Registry of Historic Places.

Designer David Becker was commissioned by DeSavary to rescue the former queen and restore her to her throne. "Becker's unparalleled reputation for perfection and attention to detail was proven with his development of our London and Antigua Clubs. He spent countless hours researching Art Deco pieces with which to furnish the Los Angeles Club and the finished product is a stunning tribute to the Art Deco period," says DeSavary about his choice.

Becker spent two years exploring the Beaux Arts Museum in Paris, the Metropolitan Museum in New York and museums in London and Italy, where the largest collections of Art Deco pieces could be found. Specially-commissioned craftsmen painstakingly reproduced Becker's selections using original veneers such as burr maple, pallisandro and faux ivory.

The care and quality of detailed workmanship is evident throughout the building. Lobby stairs were carved from a single block of Italian marble rather than being pieced together with seams. An exact replica of the chandelier, which once adorned the entrance to the Sunset Tower, was handmade of imported crystal and coated with three layers of silver. Dutch artist Peter Van Sambeek hand-painted the ceiling designs.

Each of the Club's 74 guestrooms and suites is handsomely appointed in Art Deco. Such classic furniture reproductions as Jacques Emile Ruhlman's gondola bed, with accompanying vanities, augment the style in each room as do desks made with 400 pieces of inlaid ivory.

Becker's fine attention to detailing is also obvious in the Members Dining Room. Soothing hues of gray and blue create an intimate atmosphere for the dining guest. A distinctly Italian influence pervades the area, from the imported hand-woven linens to the silverware from designer Ricci and china created by Ginori. In the Members Lounge, a mural painted by English artist Sue Lloyd features portraits of some of the Club's renowned guests—Elizabeth Taylor, Sir John Mills, Angela Lansbury, Laurence Olivier and others.

The designer's painstaking research and selection of Art Deco's finest has recreated the feeling of an era gone by. Becker is certainly correct when he says, "The St. James's Club is destined to serve as a living legacy to the legend of Hollywood."

Lobby stairs are carved from a single block of Italian marble (after).

Lobby (before).

The smooth gray exterior is offset by plaster friezes depicting the "Age of Travel" (after).

A flowered canopy hovers
over the Terrace Room for
a lovely splash of color (after).

Terrace Room (before).

Library (before)

*The Library is a showcase
of Art Deco reproductions (after).*

Hyatt Regency St. Louis Hotel
(St. Louis Union Station)

St. Louis, Missouri, USA

Project location
St. Louis, Missouri USA

Hotel company
Oppenheimer Properties

Interior design
Hirsch Bedner & Associates—Howard Pharr/*Project Director,* **Celeste White Becker; ADM Associates**

Architecture
Hellmuth, Obata & Kassabaum, Inc.

Lighting
Jules Fisher & Paul Marantz, Inc. (consultant); Albert Jaspers & Sons; JDA (consultant); Louis Baldinger & Sons (custom)

Floor covering
Tai Ping (*area carpets*); **Jack Lenor Larsen**

Photography
Jaime Ardilles-Arce

Rare is the restoration project which is of such magnitude and perfection that it sets a standard to which others aspire. The St. Louis Union Station is just such a case. It is, perhaps, the largest mixed-use rehabilitation project ever attempted in the United States. And at U.S. $135 million, certainly one of the most expensive.

Built at the end of the 19th century, The St. Louis Union Station served as a crossroads railway terminal linking the East and West coasts of America. By 1940 it had become the world's busiest train station, handling 100,000 passengers per day.

Theodore Link, the original architect, designed the complex in three segments—the Headhouse, where the ticketing counters, restaurant and management offices were located; the Midway, where travelers awaited arriving and departing trains; and the largest single span Train Shed in the world.

A century later, in October 1978, with trains no longer considered the choice mode of transportation, the last train pulled out of the St. Louis Union Station, and with it an era of glorious travel. The architects at Hellmuth, Obata & Kassabaum, Inc. were faced with restoring a facility which had fallen on hard times and finally into disrepair.

HOK's plan had to address the dilemma of building a commercial center inside a National Historic Landmark. The challenge was to integrate the dichotomous functions of a hotel and a retail mall, within a structure initially built to house trains. Moreover, nothing was to destroy the essential character of the building.

The solution came with the decision to build a "town" within the complex. Streets and parks would serve as links between the hotel and market activities. All three components were incorporated into the project. The Headhouse, with its newly restored 230-foot clock tower,

houses a portion of the Hyatt Regency St. Louis Hotel (originally the Omni International). The Midway now serves as the center of the retail complex, while the Train Shed umbrellas a 550-room hotel.

Even though HOK was essentially in charge of the overall architectural reconstruction of the entire facility, designers at the Atlanta office of Hirsch/Bedner & Associates were commissioned to restore and redesign areas of the hotel and the Gothic Corridor. Because most of the hotel was a new construction, it was important to blend classical forms of design with the structure's Gothic and Romanesque architecture.

Upon entering the Grand Hall, one is overwhelmed by the enormous barrel-vaulted ceiling, which was restored in color tones almost indistinguishable from the original palette. Passing through the hall's arches, focus is immediately drawn to two dragons depicted on an early 19th century embroidered Japanese Tapestry hanging behind the registration desk. In the Gothic Corridor, guests can relax in wing back chairs, enjoy table games or listen to sounds from the grand piano.

Elaborate draperies and oversized furniture helped scale down the 10-foot ceilings and colossal windows in the 70 suites located in the Headhouse. Art Deco and Art Noveau decor, displayed in pink, blue, red and beige color tones, were selected for room interiors.

Today, the transformation of the St. Louis Union Station stands as a testimonial to the creativity and craftsmanship of its designers, both past and present.

Renovated hotel atrium, formerly the lobby of the hotel (after).

Skylight well and staircase lobby (before).

View of the Headhouse and Clock Tower at twilight (after). (photo by Burt Glinn)

A 19th century Japanese embroidered tapestry accents the registration desk area (after).

Hotel rooms integrated into the "Midway" retail corridor under the Train Shed roof (after).

Under the Train Shed, 1982 (before).

Allegorical stained glass window over the main entrance to the Grand Hall (after).

The beautifully restored barrel-vaulted ceiling of the Grand Hall serves as the focal point of the Headhouse (after).

Window details in the Grand Hall (after).

The Grand Hall in the Headhouse (before).

Gothic Corridor in hotel (before).

The renovated space of the Gothic Corridor links the dining room with the Grand Hall, now a bar/lounge (after).

Ballroom prefunction area view toward the Grand Staircase (after).

Rich wood paneling and Art Deco light fixtures add character to the dining room, located between the meeting room area and the lobby (after).

The sitting room/dining area of the Presidential Suite (after).

Hotel Villa Magna

Madrid, Spain

Project location
Madrid, Spain

Interior design
Richmond Designs Ltd.; Tapiceria Gancedo; Sontillana; Wenceslao Garcia

Furniture
Sontillana

Photography
No credit given

The era of prosperity spawned by Spain's commercial and cultural renaissance of the mid-'70s also sparked a revival in its hotel industry. As business travelers increased, a demand for state-of-the-art accommodations generated a healthy competition amongst hoteliers. This resulted in an upgrading of properties throughout the country.

The Hotel Villa Magna, considered to be one of Madrid's finest, began an extensive renovation program in January 1988 to add a stylish new look to 200 bedrooms, suites and public areas. Its location, on the grounds of the former patrician Palacio de Larios, dotted with century-old cedar trees and lush gardens, mandated that an aristocratic image be maintained.

The contract for the interior redesign of the property was awarded to British-based Richmond Designs Ltd. Their reputation in restorative design answered the hotel's refurbishment needs. The design team chose modern classicism as their central design theme in order to preserve Villa Magna's traditional atmosphere.

An aura of casual elegance greets visitors as they step into the lobby. Marble floors and columns combine to evoke a palatial setting.

Upon entering the main lounge, attention is quickly drawn to the hotel's new granite and oak Champagne Bar, set off to one side on a marble platform. A chic atmosphere and a selection of more than 100 French and Spanish champagnes have made it a popular meeting point in Madrid.

Conference rooms, furnished in rich mahogany, offer a refined business-like atmosphere. Unlike many hotels whose meeting facilities are located below ground level, Villa Magna's are located above, allowing guests a view of its surrounding landscape.

In the Rue Royale restaurant, lattice-work screens, translucent curtains, and full-length mirrored walls draped with tapestries were used by the design team to elicit stately luxury and old-world charm.

After the nine-month, U.S. $17 million rehabilitation of the 5-star Hotel Villa Magna, the Richmond Design Group can add another feather to its cap, while Madrid adds another diamond to its tiara of grand hotels.

Entrance to hotel (before).

A revolving door was
added to the new
entrance; a colorfully
patterned carpet lends
spark and definition to the
sitting area (after).

Walls were refinished in a cream color, with matching furniture and carpeting creating a refreshing new look for the lobby lounge (after).

Lobby lounge (before).

Typical guestroom (before).

*Delicately textured fabrics
in blue and mauve lend a
stately elegance to the
typical guestroom (after).*

Old Mayfair Bar before conversion into the new Mayfair Conference Room.

Rich mahogany finishes echo the business-like atmosphere of the Mayfair Conference Room (after).

Restaurant (before).

To promote an airy, garden-like atmosphere in the new restaurant, old wall murals were removed (after).

The Westin Bayshore

Vancouver, B.C., Canada

Project location
Vancouver, B.C. Canada

Lighting
Alan R. Daly Ltd.; Gen-Light Ltd.; Johnson-Lazare Canada Inc.

Furniture
Barrymore Furniture Co.; W.D. Designers Upholstery

Floor covering
Barrymore Carpet Co.

Photography
No credit given

Resort hotels are expected to be surrounded by acres of woodlands, or lie adjacent to bodies of water—their popularity defined by the recreational facilities offered (i.e., tennis courts, golf courses, skiing, etc.). Seldom is a resort located in the heart of a metropolis.

The 519-room Westin Bayshore boasts all of the above, and more, in an unusual urban setting. Looking out the front of the hotel, Coal Harbor is seen spilling into the Burrard Inlet. The back of the property is encompassed by the 1,000-acre Stanley Park, the largest in Vancouver. A mere two miles away lies Grouse Mountain, where skiers flock to try out their skills.

FORMA, Westin's inhouse design group, was handed the responsibility of overseeing The Westin Bayshore's recent U.S. $10 million renovation. This was accomplished in four phases over a three-year period. The first two facets included the remodeling of guestrooms and suites, the third was a refurbishment of the public spaces and conference facilities, and the last segment supplied a facelift to the adjacent 18-story Tower Building.

Guestrooms were designed to reflect a comfortable, casual resort atmosphere while still offering facilities to accommodate the business traveler. A more formal, elegant style was chosen for the suites which are used both as hospitality spaces and private residences. Flexible furniture arrangements, with a selection of luxurious materials and colors, in soft pastels, added to the grace and comfort of these areas.

An eclectic international decor was chosen for the award-winning International Suite. An ambience, characteristic of an old English country house, is reflected in the paisley and brown finishes of its second bedroom. A large Asian screen, positioned against one of the walls, divulges the Oriental influence of Vancouver's Pacific community.

The public corridors—previously long and dark—were brightened and visually shortened with bordered area rugs, custom lighting and subtle color variations. Continuity of design was carried from the lobby into the ballroom and meeting spaces with new carpeting and furnishings. The casual elegance the design team strived for was achieved and well-received.

If the city's founder, British explorer Captain George Vancouver, were alive today, he could not choose a better place to rest and relax than The Westin Bayshore.

The fabric enveloping the four-poster bed perks up the pastel-toned surroundings in the main bedroom (after).

Furniture is comfortable yet elegant, promoting a relaxed feeling in the main salon of the International Suite (after).

Brown and paisley finishes, reminiscent of an English country house, are offset by the Asian screen in background (after).

The Wigwam Resort and Country Club

Litchfield Park, Arizona, USA

Project location
Litchfield Park, Arizona, USA

Hotel company
Suncor Development Company, a subsidiary of Pinnacle West Capital Corporation

Interior design
Cole Martinez Curtis and Associates—Jill Cole/*Project Executive*; **Michael King**/*Project Director*, **Rikki Dallow**/*Project Designer*, **Colleen Neilson**/*Designer*

Architecture
Allen & Philp Architects, Inc.; Sheperd, Nelson & Wheeler

Furniture
A. Rudin (*Sun Lounge, Kachina Lounge*); **Murray's Iron Works** (*Sun Lounge, Kachina Lounge, Arizona kitchen, Terrace Dining Room, Palm Room—chandeliers*); **Beverly Interiors Stewart Furniture Manufacturing, Inc.** (*Sun Lounge, Arizona kitchen, Fairway Casa guestroom, guestroom bar, bath and living room*)

Lighting
LA-Spec Lighting Industries, Inc. (*Sachem Hall*); **Hinkley's Lighting Co.** (*Sun Lounge and Kachina Lounge—reworked cowbell sconces and reworked existing beanpot chandeliers*); **Thomas W. Morgan** (*Sun Lounge, Kachina Lounge*); **Paul Ferrante** (*Sun Lounge, Kachina Lounge, Arizona kitchen, Terrace dining room*); **Ron Rezek** (*Fairway Casa guestroom, guestroom bar*); **Hallmark Lighting** (*Fairway Casa guestroom, guestroom bath and livingroom, Tennis Casita*)

Wall Treatment
J.M. Lynne Co. (*Sachem Hall*); **Wall-Pride, Inc.** (*guestroom bath*)

Floor covering
Sewelson's Carpets International (*custom-designed area rugs, Sun Lounge, Kachina Lounge*)

Photography
Toshi Yoshimi

The Wigwam Resort and Country Club has had an ongoing symbiotic relationship with Litchfield Park, Arizona for the last 70 years. The town itself was named after Paul Litchfield, the one-time president and board chairman of the Goodyear Tire and Rubber Company. His development of a new tire, made of a locally grown cotton fiber, initiated the company's relationship with the community.

In 1919, an "Organization House" was built to house Goodyear sales representatives and business associates. The two-story adobe structure eventually became the social center of Litchfield Park and was opened to the public in 1929 as the Wigwam Resort.

Over the years, a series of low-rise, adobe-style casitas were added to the property, evoking images of a Spanish hacienda. Eventually, a country club, golf course and swimming pool were incorporated into the resort. By 1987, the 13-room lodging facility had grown to over 200 rooms.

Its new owners, Suncor Development Company, contracted the well-respected design firm, Cole Martinez Curtis and Associates, to upgrade their new purchase.

Suncor insisted on preserving Wigwam's historical quality by recreating its original Southwestern style while maintaining its refined sophistication.

Jill Cole, a principal with the California-based design company, set about interweaving the territorial Southwest and its Indian influences with modern technology. She comments, "We even wanted the 'new' construction to look as if it could have been built in the Twenties." Many of the original design elements were repeated and others saved for use in new public spaces.

The warm and cozy Fireplace Lounge was converted from the resort's former registration lobby. Old "bean pot" chandeliers were spruced up, and now contribute to the room's illumination. By adding Indian-patterned area rugs, the designers were able to reinforce the Southwestern-look in the lobby.

The custom-designed river rock bar in the Kachina Lounge, topped with hammered copper, suggests a decidedly "Western" ambience. Overstuffed furniture and well-displayed regional artifacts continue the feeling of rustic elegance and intimacy.

The Arizona Kitchen, one of the property's two restaurants, resembles an old home kitchen. Stucco walls, brick floor and a wooden ceiling serve as a perfect backdrop for the regional fare offered.

Two color schemes define the guestrooms at The Wigwam. The blue scheme is accented by terra cotta, green and cinnamon, while turquoise, lavender and orange complement the adobe scheme. In some of the rooms, shutters are used as substitutes for draperies. Again, Indian-patterned fabrics and artwork complete the Southwest decor.

Even the 6,000 trees found on the property cannot cast a shadow over the popularity of this world-class resort.

Indian spear detail in Sun Lounge (after).

Sun Lounge (before).

Bench detail in Sun Lounge (after).

Indian artifact in Sun Lounge (after)

Doors, with a god's eye motif, provide an unencumbered view of the swimming pool patio from the Sun Lounge (after).

Kachina Lounge bar area (before).

"Bean pot" chandelier detail (after).

A custom-designed river rock bar with a hammered copper top is the main feature of the Kachina Lounge (after).

The Fireplace Lounge, formerly the registration lobby, provides a cozy, homey atmosphere for relaxation (after).

Patrons of the Arizona Kitchen Restaurant can casually watch their food being prepared in the exhibition kitchen, characterized by terra cotta-colored tile walls and checkerboard counter top (after).

Swimming pool (before).

Outdoor chair detail—
Terrace Dining Room (after).

A fire pit has been added to the swimming pool area to warm up swimmers during cool Arizona evenings (after).

A palette of terra cotta, green and cinnamon add a bright cheerfulness to the Fairway Casa guestroom (after).

Wood-paneled walls, a tiled counter top and window shutters portray a home-like environment in the bar area of guestroom (after).

Typical guestroom (before).

Ballroom (before).

New lighting and desert earth tones (in the carpeting, stage curtain and seating) create an elegantly subdued ambience in Sachem Hall (ballroom) (after).

Functional fireplaces imbue the living room areas with an aura of warmth and coziness (after).

A mirror at the side of the
wash basin optically
enlarges the space in the
guestroom bath (after).

Typical guestroom bath (before).

INDEX

FLOOR COVERING

FURNITURE

HOTEL COMPANIES

INTERIOR DESIGN

WALL COVERING

DATE DUE

MAR 2 0 1991		
APR 0 8 1992		
DEC 2 3 1992		
MAY 0 7 1997		
MAY 0 7 199		
AUG 2 1 1997		
MAY 0 5 1998		
MAY 1 2 1999		
APR 2.1 1999		
MAY 1 2 1999		
MAR 1 4 2000		